Shaun White

Other books in the People in the News series:

Adele
Maya Angelou
David Beckham
Beyoncé
Justin Bieber
Sandra Bullock
Fidel Castro
Kelly Clarkson
Hillary Clinton
George Clooney
Stephen Colbert
Suzanne Collins
Natalie Coughlin
Miley Cyrus
Ellen Degeneres
Johnny Depp
Eminem
Roger Federer
50 Cent
James Franco
Glee Cast and Creators
Jeff Gordon
Anne Hathaway
Tony Hawk
Salma Hayek
Jennifer Hudson
LeBron James
Jay-Z
Wyclef Jean
Derek Jeter
Steve Jobs
Dwayne Johnson

Alicia Keys
Kim Jong Il
Coretta Scott King
Taylor Lautner
Spike Lee
George Lopez
Jennifer Lopez
Eli Manning
Stephenie Meyer
Nicki Minaj
Barack Obama
Michelle Obama
Apolo Anton Ohno
Danica Patrick
Katy Perry
Tyler Perry
Prince Harry
Condoleezza Rice
Rihanna
Alex Rodriguez
Derrick Rose
J.K. Rowling
Shakira
Kelly Slater
Taylor Swift
Justin Timberlake
Usher
Lindsey Vonn
Denzel Washington
Serena Williams
Oprah Winfrey
Mark Zuckerberg

Shaun White

By Christine Wilcox

LUCENT BOOKS
A part of Gale, Cengage Learning

GALE
CENGAGE Learning·

Detroit • New York • San Francisco • New Haven, Conn • Waterville, Maine • London

Library of Congress Cataloging-in-Publication Data

Wilcox, Christine.
    Shaun White / by Christine Wilcox.
        pages cm. -- (People in the news)
    Includes bibliographical references and index.
    ISBN 978-1-4205-0891-8 (hardcover)
1. White, Shaun, 1986---Juvenile literature. 2. Snowboarders--United
States--Biography--Juvenile literature. I. Title.
    GV857.S57W55575 2013
    796.939092--dc23
    [B]
                                                        2012050538

Lucent Books
27500 Drake Rd
Farmington Hills MI 48331

ISBN-13: 978-1-4205-0891-8
ISBN-10: 1-4205-0891-1

Printed in the United States of America
1 2 3 4 5 6 7 17 16 15 14 13

Contents

Fame and celebrity are alluring. People are drawn to those who walk in fame's spotlight, whether they are known for great accomplishments or for notorious deeds. The lives of the famous pique public interest and attract attention, perhaps because their experiences seem in some ways so different from, yet in other ways so similar to, our own.

Newspapers, magazines, and television regularly capitalize on this fascination with celebrity by running profiles of famous people. For example, television programs such as *Entertainment Tonight* devote all their programming to stories about entertainment and entertainers. Magazines such as *People* fill their pages with stories of the private lives of famous people. Even newspapers, newsmagazines, and television news frequently delve into the lives of well-known personalities. Despite the number of articles and programs, few provide more than a superficial glimpse at their subjects.

Lucent's People in the News series offers young readers a deeper look into the lives of today's newsmakers, the influences that have shaped them, and the impact they have had in their fields of endeavor and on other people's lives. The subjects of the series hail from many disciplines and walks of life. They include authors, musicians, athletes, political leaders, entertainers, entrepreneurs, and others who have made a mark on modern life and who, in many cases, will continue to do so for years to come.

These biographies are more than factual chronicles. Each book emphasizes the contributions, accomplishments, or deeds that have brought fame or notoriety to the individual and shows how that person has influenced modern life. Authors portray their subjects in a realistic, unsentimental light. For example, Bill Gates—cofounder of the software giant Microsoft—has been instrumental in making personal computers the most vital tool of the modern age. Few dispute his business savvy, his perseverance, or his technical expertise, yet critics say he is ruthless in his dealings with competitors and driven more by his desire to maintain Microsoft's dominance in the computer industry than by an interest in furthering technology.

In these books, young readers will encounter inspiring stories about real people who achieved success despite enormous obstacles. Oprah Winfrey—one of the most powerful, most watched, and wealthiest women in television history—spent the first six years of her life in the care of her grandparents while her unwed mother sought work and a better life elsewhere. Her adolescence was colored by pregnancy at age fourteen, rape, and sexual abuse.

Each author documents and supports his or her work with an array of primary and secondary source quotations taken from diaries, letters, speeches, and interviews. All quotes are footnoted to show readers exactly how and where biographers derive their information and provide guidance for further research. The quotations enliven the text by giving readers eyewitness views of the life and accomplishments of each person covered in the People in the News series.

In addition, each book in the series includes photographs, annotated bibliographies, timelines, and comprehensive indexes. For both the casual reader and the student researcher, the People in the News series offers insight into the lives of today's newsmakers—people who shape the way we live, work, and play in the modern age.

The Flying Tomato

To sports fans the world over, the name Shaun White is synonymous with snowboarding. The two-time Olympic gold medalist is the most successful snowboarder in the history of the sport, earning more than $10 million a year in competition prizes and endorsement deals. Also a top professional skateboarder, his competition record is a series of "firsts"—he was the first to compete in both the summer and winter X Games; he is the only athlete to win both the summer and winter Dew Cup; and he is the first person to successfully land a host of extremely complex snowboarding and skateboarding tricks, including two of his own invention—the double McTwist 1260 and the Armadillo. As snowboarding's most vocal—and most recognizable—advocate, his dynamic performances have brought the sport into the mainstream of popular culture.

A Young Talent

Named after world champion surfer Shaun Tomson, White has been riding boards since he was four years old—first a boogie board in the California surf, then a skateboard on his brother's ramp in the backyard, and finally a snowboard. He was so talented that, at seven years old, his parents entered him in his first amateur snowboarding contest, which he won. At thirteen, he turned pro, competing against snowboarding legends like Terje Haakonsen. At the time, snowboarding was thought of as a fringe sport, and his parents never imagined their son could one day make a living as a professional snowboarder. They supported him anyway, pinching pennies by sleeping in a camper van outside of the ski resorts in eastern California and, later, putting their own lives on hold to accompany him to international events.

Even with the support of his family, White's childhood was "lonely and strange."[1] He was much younger than the other competitors, whom he fondly described as "gnarly ruffians . . . on a mission of destruction."[2] His fame made school difficult for him; his peers either accused him of being stuck up or they pestered him for free sports equipment. In addition, his school would not give him any course credit for the time he spent competing—not even for physical education. His grades suffered so much that his parents moved him to a school with an independent study program that encouraged real-world study of other countries and cultures.

Not Just a Snowboarder

Nicknamed "The Flying Tomato" by his mentor, skateboarder Tony Hawk, White went pro in skateboarding at fifteen. He competed in the X Games in his very first year, which was unheard of in pro skating. Even though he was extremely talented, many seasoned riders felt he should have paid his dues in the amateur circuit. They also resented that he already had a lucrative career as a snowboarder, and that he turned pro in skating just because he was "having so much fun with it."[3] He eventually gained their respect by winning two gold medals in the X Games vert competition, beating legends like Bucky Lasek and Pierre-Luc Gagnon.

Still, White sometimes felt like an outsider in the skateboarding community, in part because he could not socialize with the other riders in the off season. He had a similar problem in the snowboarding community. "It's hard to hang with the other guys," he said. "I think differently from most of them, have a different life."[4]

A Media Favorite

White became a national icon after he won the gold medal in the 2006 Olympic snowboarding competition. The media loved him; he was articulate, thoughtful, and always happy to promote his sport. Corporations loved him as well—his long red hair made him instantly recognizable. He was soon flooded with endorsement offers for everything from computers to ketchup. He rejected the ones that turned snowboarding into a joke or portrayed snowboarders as slackers who called each other "dude" and "bro." It was important to him that snowboarding get positive media exposure. Exposure meant more new riders, which in turn meant better snowboard parks at ski resorts. "It just helps make better riders for the future," he said. "It just inspires more kids."[5]

White's exceptional athletic skills, distinctive look, and media savvy have made him a hit with sponsors and fans alike.

The Double Cork

To prepare for the 2010 Olympics, White trained at a secret site deep in the Colorado backcountry, where energy beverage maker Red Bull had built a halfpipe specifically for White's use. There, he developed controversial and dangerous double cork maneuvers, which involve multiple spins and flips over the lip of the halfpipe. At the 2010 Olympics, he stunned the crowd with the double McTwist 1260, a trick that combined two flips and three and a half revolutions. No one had ever done a double cork in competition before, and White's use of the trick pushed the sport into new territory. Because of his innovative work, double corks are now commonplace in professional snowboarding competitions.

Now in his twenties, White is entering his peak as a professional athlete, and he is busy transitioning into the next stage of his life. He was a commentator at the 2012 Summer Olympics, and he recently started a skateboard manufacturing company. He competes every chance he gets, and he hopes to compete in future Olympic Games. Regardless of what he chooses to do next, he will be in the public eye for many years to come.

Chapter 1

A Born Competitor

Roger and Cathy White were not typical parents. Roger had been an avid longboard surfer for years, and Cathy had struck out on her own to Hawaii when she was still a teenager. They lived near the beach in San Diego, California, and when they were not surfing, they were skiing on Mammoth Mountain, in central California. Living life to the fullest meant everything to the Whites. So when their third son, Shaun, had to endure two dangerous surgeries to correct an abnormality in his heart, they had a choice: they could try to protect him from the world, or they could teach him to savor everything it had to offer.

Tetralogy of Fallot

On September 3, 1986, Roger and Cathy White welcomed their third child into the world: Shaun Roger White. Like all new parents, they had big dreams for their son. They named him after Shaun Tomson, the world-champion surfer, and Roger could not wait to buy his son his first surfboard. The Whites had two other children: Kari, who was a year old when Shaun was born, and Jesse, who was seven. Jesse was showing great promise as an athlete, and Roger and Cathy had no doubt that both Kari and Shaun would follow in Jesse's footsteps.

Shortly after Shaun's birth, the Whites' dreams turned into a parent's worst nightmare. Their baby had been born with a congenital heart defect called tetralogy of Fallot. Shaun's heart had not formed properly in the womb, and there were several holes between its right and left ventricles—the chambers that pump blood throughout the body. Because of this, oxygenated and deoxygenated blood mixed together, and Shaun was not getting enough oxygen. If his heart was not repaired, it was very likely he would die before he reached the age of twenty.

The Whites were devastated. Shaun needed two dangerous open-heart surgeries—one to help increase blood flow through his heart, and the other to repair his heart permanently. He had his first surgery at about six months of age, and his second less than a year later. During this difficult time, Roger and Cathy struggled to make ends meet while simultaneously caring for a very sick baby and his active siblings. They were not wealthy— Roger worked for the San Clemente Water Department and Cathy waited tables—so money was extremely tight. Luckily, the hospital that performed Shaun's surgeries allowed the whole family to move into a care facility nearby, allowing Roger and Cathy to stay close to all three of their children.

"We Don't Take Anything for Granted"

The surgeries were a success, and Shaun's prognosis was excellent. However, while he was encouraged to exercise and to play sports, it was important that he did not push himself to the limits of his endurance because his heart might not be able to pump enough blood through his body. Also, if he injured himself, which is quite common in the extreme sports field, he could not have an MRI (a common diagnostic test that uses strong magnets to create images of the inside of the body) because two metal leads had been placed in his heart just in case he needed a pacemaker in the future. Even though none of these issues would prevent him from living a normal, active life, there was a chance that he would not be as active in sports as the rest of his family.

Whereas most parents would have become overprotective of a child who had nearly died before his first birthday, Shaun's parents reacted quite differently. Roger and Cathy decided they would not let Shaun's condition stop him from pursuing his dreams. "It made us realize how short life is, how precious your children are," Cathy

White celebrates his victory at the 2010 U.S. Snowboarding Grand Prix with his mother, Cathy, left, and father, Roger. The Whites urged their three children to pursue their dreams and live life to the fullest.

said about the ordeal. "We don't take anything for granted."[6] The Whites wanted all of their children to live life to the fullest, so they decided to treat Shaun no differently than his siblings. "My parents never made it into something that I needed to worry about," he says about his childhood heart condition. "Can you imagine my parents going through all of that stuff [when I was] that age and then going, 'Cool, go snowboarding, go skateboarding.' I mean, what an amazing household to be in where your parents are that supportive of whatever you want to do."[7]

Wild Child

As well as having a congenital heart condition, Shaun was also born bowlegged. To straighten his legs, he had to wear corrective braces at night for the first few years of his life. Even so, he was an extremely active child. His favorite story was Rudyard Kipling's *The Jungle Book*, and he loved to climb on things like the book's main character, Mowgli, a boy who was raised by wolves in the Indian jungle. His mother worried about him all the time, but she tried her best not to let it show. "He always had the desire to hang on the edge," she remembers. "I'd take him to the zoo, and he'd walk on top of the rocks, teetering over the lions' cage. We'd go to the pier to look at the waves, and he'd stand on the railing, hanging off the side with no hands."[8] Shaun recalls that even as a young boy, he was always on a mission to do something unusual or thrilling or shocking, which made life very difficult for his parents. "I was a monster," he remembers, "a problem child."[9]

When Shaun was four, his parents took him on a vacation to a ski resort. Skiing seemed like a good fit for Shaun—it was not an endurance sport that would exhaust him and overtax his heart, and it was something that the whole family could enjoy together. Shaun took to skiing immediately. He had no fear of falling; all he wanted to do was keep up with Jesse, whom he idolized. His parents had a hard time controlling Shaun. "I kept hitting other people with the poles,"[10] he remembers. Finally his parents had to take away his ski poles altogether. Without poles, Shaun quickly learned how to balance himself so he could keep up with Jesse, developing skills that would serve him well later.

A Boy on a Board

By the time Jesse White was a teenager, he was a skilled skateboarder—so of course, six-year-old Shaun wanted to skateboard as well. Many people regard skateboarding as more dangerous than snowboarding, especially since one falls a lot. "The slightest flick of your foot or gust of wind can send your board flying,"[11] Shaun explained. Despite the risks, his parents got Shaun a skateboard. He practiced on Jesse's skateboard ramp in the backyard, and tagged along with his brother to the Encinitas YMCA, which had an area specially designed for skateboarders.

That winter, Jesse took up another sport—snowboarding. Shaun was eager to try it, and his parents agreed, mainly because

Jesse White, left, attends a media event in 2011 with his brother. Jesse's interest and skill in skateboarding and snowboarding as a teenager inspired his younger brother to try the sports himself.

they thought a snowboard would slow Shaun down. "He was crazy on skis," his mother remembers. "And so I thought, 'Well, we'll put him on a snowboard and he'll fall all the time, and I won't have to worry about trying to dig him out of trees.'"[12] Snowboarding lessons were only for children twelve and older, so Roger decided he would take a lesson and then teach Shaun. While his dad was taking his lesson, however, Shaun grabbed his new snowboard and followed Jesse up—and then down— the mountain, determined to do what his older brother was doing. Because he knew how to skateboard, he got the hang of snowboarding right away. "As soon as he started snowboarding, he started jumping," his mother remembers. "He took off. We couldn't believe it."[13]

"I'm Never Doing This Again"

When Shaun was about six, his father took him surfing for the very first time. It was a cold, windy day in California, and the waves were huge, but Roger thought his daredevil son, who had been riding a boogie board since he was four, was up to the challenge. "He took me out and set me out on this giant wave that I wasn't ready for," Shaun remembers, recounting the story in a rush. "I go under and get swirled around. It's cold and I'm in a spring [wet]suit and I'm getting swirled

White rides a wave in Hawaii in 2011.

around and I come up for air and I don't get it and get swirled more and finally come up and the board just smacks me in the face. I'm bleeding, and I'm sitting there like . . . I'm never doing this again.'" His father, who had dreamed of that day for years, just shrugged. After all, surfing was supposed to be fun.

Shaun was too afraid to try surfing again until he was thirteen. It is now one of his favorite hobbies.

Quoted in Robert Wilonsky. "Chairman of the Board." *American Way*, January 1, 2012. www.americanwaymag.com/shaun-tomson-shaun-white-pacific-ocean.

"If I Did Well, I Would Get New Boards"

Soon, the whole family was snowboarding. Jesse and his friends—all much older than Shaun—liked to ride through the snowboard park in a group, and Shaun followed behind. "There would be

The name of snowboard maker Burton is visible during White's halfpipe run at a competition in 2008. Anticipating White's future success, Burton became his sponsor when he was still a young boy.

six or seven of us," he remembers, "with the best guy in the front and I'm in the very back. But if you're travelling the same speed as everyone else, you're going to make it over the jumps. I'd be going off these huge hits and I wouldn't even really know it. It gave me so much confidence."[14] Shaun's confidence was well deserved—with Jesse's help, he was quickly becoming an expert snowboarder.

Shaun was so talented that, when he was seven, his parents decided to enter him in his first amateur contest. Snowboarding was just beginning to gain popularity, though it was still seen as an outlaw sport; snowboarders were thought to be irresponsible risk-takers, and many ski resorts either banned snowboarding altogether or had only a single snowboard run, set far away from the ski trails. However, there were still opportunities to compete, and Shaun was excited to try. His parents entered him into the Southern California Collegiate Snowsports Conference's annual competition, and Shaun won his first contest. And he kept winning. He made it all the way to the national championships that year, finishing in eleventh place in the twelve-and-under category.

His performance caught the attention of Burton Snowboards. Burton was the first company to manufacture snowboards, and today it is the largest snowboard brand in the world. It offered to sponsor Shaun, betting that he would one day become a well-known pro snowboarder. Burton was just coming out with a line of snowboards for children, and they offered to make him a board. This was a huge motivator for Shaun, who had no interest in the fame and money that sponsorship could lead to. "All I knew was that if I did well, I would get new boards."[15]

"When The Pressure Was There, I Would Do Better"

After making it to the nationals, Shaun realized that he loved contests. He wanted to continue to compete—not because it fed his ego, but because he liked pushing himself. He thrived on competition, quite the opposite of his brother Jesse. "I wasn't better than him," Shaun said of Jesse's snowboarding skills. "It was just that I was better at contests for some reason. When the pressure was there, I would do better. But if there was any kind of pressure, it wasn't his thing, he wouldn't do as well, or he'd get nervous. Some people are just good at contests, and at a certain point I passed him."[16]

Shaun deeply admired Jesse's snowboarding skills, but he was also fiercely competitive when it came to Jesse. While he was usually content to simply compete against himself—at least when it came to sports—he was obsessed with beating his brother. In fact, he believes that Jesse played a big part in making him such a fierce competitor. When asked about his need to be the best, Shaun said, "I think it's from years of playing board games with my older brother. He always wins. I wanted to win so bad. And that one time that I'm about to win, he kicks the board or something and doesn't give me the satisfaction."[17] Though Jesse was far less competitive, he never missed an opportunity to put his little brother in his place. Still, Shaun credits his early skill to Jesse. "He's the one that inspires me the most," White says. "I'd just ride with my bro and get better and better."[18]

In the early nineties, snowboarding was a young sport. There were very few opportunities to compete on a professional level and even fewer opportunities for spectators to watch snowboarders do their spectacular aerial tricks. Shaun's parents assumed that, even if their son became the best snowboarder in the world, he would never have the financial success of a pro football or basketball player. But true to the promise they had made to themselves when Shaun was a baby, they supported his ambition to be a top snowboard competitor.

After Shaun's success at the Snowsports Conference, his parents began helping him train in earnest. Cathy often took Shaun out of school and drove him to the mountains in the middle of the week. Roger arrived on Friday with Kari and Jesse, allowing Cathy to return to Carlsbad to wait tables on Saturday night. Sometimes Cathy or Roger even called in sick to work, just so they could take Shaun to the mountains to practice. Their sacrifices paid off; the next year, when Shaun was eight, he once again entered the Snowsports Conference amateur competition. This time he not only made it to nationals but won the national championship. It was the first of five consecutive wins at the conference, and the start of a spectacular amateur career.

"It Was a Weird Time"

Shaun does not have happy memories from his early years in school. When he first began competing, most people had no idea what snowboarding was, and none of the other kids understood why he was out of school so much. "I didn't have any friends," he remembers. "It was a weird time."[1] His teachers did not understand why his parents would let their son participate in such a dangerous sport, and the Whites had to endure a lot of criticism and ridicule from other parents. None of this got in the way of Shaun's dreams. When he was competing in the 2010 Winter Dew Tour, a reporter asked: "When you were a little kid, did you ever picture you'd be where you are now?" He responded, "You know honestly, to be dead honest, I did. I wanted to be here, I wanted to be the best in these sports, I wanted all of that. It's such a bizarre thing to walk through this life right now and be there. . . . When you're that young, your dreams are so close. I just went for them."[2]

[1.] Quoted in Sportskool. "One on One with Shaun White." HBO, 2008. Streamed online via Grace Creek Media. www.sportskool.com/sports/snowboarding.
[2.] Quoted in FM News Radio 750 KXL. "Olympian Shaun White," August 12, 2010. www .youtube.com/user/750kxl/videos?query=shaun+white.

Roughing It

Between equipment, resort fees, and travel, it cost the Whites twenty thousand dollars a year for Shaun to compete. To save money on their trips to the mountains, they either slept in their camper van (a 1964 Econoline they nicknamed "Big Mo"), or they piled into a single motel room. When they camped, they had to take makeshift showers at rest stops, filling used milk cartons with hot water from the sink and pouring it over themselves. They cooked their meals on a portable stove—either in the van or in the room they all shared. "We were cooking in the room and the fire alarm went off," Shaun remembers. "My brother and sister and I had to hide in the bathtub [when the manager came], because you can't have that many people in a room."[19] At the time, Shaun had no idea there was anything wrong with what his family was doing, and saw all of it as a big adventure.

Ski resorts are notoriously expensive places, and the Whites did not fit in with the other families, whose children had fancy equipment and personal coaches. In addition, lift tickets are expensive, and there were times when Shaun had to hike up the mountain, rather than ride the lift, to participate in a competition. "We prided ourselves with being more ghetto," Shaun says of how the family dealt with the snobbery they encountered. "I remember that my dad stuck a pizza box over the radiator (of our van)—it kept the heat in, or something. We get to this super-fancy upper-class ski resort, and some lady came out and said, 'You can't park *that thing* here.' So my mom leans out of the car and says, 'Hey, honey, take that pizza box off the radiator!'"[20]

Team White

The more Shaun snowboarded, the more he realized that he preferred solo sports over team sports. For instance, despite his heart condition, he had become a talented soccer player and loved the game; however, he disliked the rigid practice schedules, preferring to practice because he wanted to, not because he had to. Also, his success on the soccer field made him stand out in an uncomfortable way. "I couldn't handle the moms," he said. "They'd yell at me because I got to play and their kid didn't."[21] He eventually dropped soccer, preferring solo sports because "you learn at your own speed. It wasn't like somebody was sitting there telling you how to do something. If you wanted advice you'd ask an older guy how to do a trick, but it wasn't like someone was sitting there reading a manual on drills."[22]

There were elements of team sports that Shaun did enjoy, however, and luckily, his family provided those. Their struggles to pinch pennies so they could afford to snowboard gave the whole family a feeling of togetherness. "It wasn't my dad yelling at me from the sideline," Shaun explained. "It was more like we were

White celebrates his halfpipe gold medal in the 2006 Winter Olympics in Turin, Italy, with his parents and siblings. The family credits snowboarding as a pursuit that drew them close to each other.

there together, riding on the mountain."[23] Shaun's family became his team, and snowboarding bonded them tightly together.

Meeting Tony Hawk

Shaun spent his summers skateboarding. He enjoyed skating both "park" (doing tricks in a concrete skate park) and skating "vert." Vert-style skateboarding entails doing tricks inside a halfpipe, a U-shaped ramp used in both snowboarding and skateboarding. (Skateboarders refer to the halfpipe they use as a "vert ramp," and it is usually made from wood or laminate; the halfpipe snowboarders use is made of compacted snow.) Soon Shaun became an accomplished vert skater, doing tricks that many older skaters dared not even try.

White poses with skateboarding legend Tony Hawk, right. Hawk became White's mentor when the boy was nine years old.

The Whites lived near the Encinitas YMCA, where pro skaters like Tony Hawk and Bob Burnquist often practiced. "These guys would . . . do these amazing tricks," Shaun recalls. "I was just so blown away."[24] It did not take long for Hawk to notice how skilled Shaun was, and when Shaun was nine, Hawk began to mentor him. The two struck up a strong friendship that has lasted to this day. "Tony and I would always talk," Shaun remembers. "He has helped me with advice and experience, which means a lot to me."[25]

Though Shaun loved to skateboard, he never competed in the amateur circuit. Skating was like a vacation from snowboarding, and he was only interested in competing against himself. Still, he was so talented that Hawk often invited him to appear in exhibitions. Shaun enjoyed performing for the crowds, and he relished being in Hawk's company.

"I Thought We Lost Him"

One such exhibition nearly ended his skateboarding—and snowboarding—career for good. When he was eleven, he was skating doubles with Bob Burnquist at the 1997 MTV Sports and Music Festival, and he crashed into Burnquist. "Our lines got messed up and we hit [in] midair,"[26] Shaun remembers. Shaun was only half the size of Burnquist, and the collision left him limp at the bottom of the vert ramp. His parents, who were watching from the sidelines, were horrified. "It was the scariest moment of my life," his mother said. "I thought we lost him."[27] Shaun had fractured his skull and broken his right hand and foot.

While he was recovering from the accident, he told his parents that he wanted to quit skateboarding for good. "I'm like, 'I hate you,'"[28] White said, remembering his feelings toward skateboarding after the accident. However, as he got stronger, he changed his mind. As soon as he was able, he threw himself into trying to master the sport that had nearly killed him. "I ended up learning a new trick because I stayed,"[29] he said. And while his mother was terrified he would hurt himself again, she continued to allow him to skate. "I think, deep down, he was afraid," she said, "but I kept taking him to the Y."[30]

Turning Pro

From the ages of seven to twelve, Shaun won almost every snowboarding contest he entered. At twelve years old, after competing in the U.S. Open as an amateur, he decided it was time to turn pro. "They freaked out when I showed up at the junior event," he remembers, referring to the parents of other young competitors, who knew their kids had no chance against Shaun. "So from that day on I said, 'Forget it, I'm gonna just enter pro.'" He turned pro at thirteen, and never looked back. "Once I was in the pro events it pushed me harder to learn new stuff," he said. "It was probably the best decision I ever made."[31]

Chapter 2

Rising Through the Ranks

In 1998, the year before Shaun White turned pro, snowboarding was included in the Olympic games for the first time. That inclusion was surrounded with controversy: Terje Haakonsen, considered at the time to be the best snowboarder in the world, boycotted the event because the Olympic Committee chose to ignore the ranking and scoring standards set by the International Snowboarding Federation (ISF). Moreover, the gold-medal winner was stripped of his title for a time because he tested positive for trace amounts of marijuana. Thirteen-year-old Shaun entered pro snowboarding during a period of growing pains, and he quickly realized the importance of being professional both on and off the snow.

Future Boy

In December 1999, Shaun entered his first professional competition: the halfpipe event at the Vans Triple Crown, held in Breckenridge, Colorado. If Shaun wanted to be challenged, he was in the right place; the Vans Triple Crown drew competitors from all over the world. The weather was perfect, and the halfpipe had 14-foot walls (4.3m) and was in excellent condition. During the qualifying runs, Shaun and fifteen-year-old Takaharu Nakai were "boosting like the big boys,"[32] getting as much height off the lip of the halfpipe as their older competitors. At one point,

Shaun ranked first in the qualifiers, much to the amazement of the crowd. He placed tenth at the event—an amazing showing for his first professional outing—and won a prize of four hundred dollars.

Shaun's mother had left her waitressing job to accompany him on tour and manage his new career. That season, he competed in halfpipe competitions at the Nippon Open in Japan (he placed third); the Sims Invitational in British Columbia, Canada (he placed fifth); and the Grand Prix in Colorado and Vermont (he placed sixteenth and fourth, respectively). Snowboarders advance to larger events according to the points they are awarded in lesser competitions. In his first season, Shaun earned enough points to compete in the winter X Games, where he came in fifteenth in the halfpipe event. He was quickly dubbed Future Boy by the media, who saw him as the most exciting up-and-comer in the sport.

First Big Win as a Pro

In his second season Shaun won his first professional contest at the prestigious Arctic Challenge in Norway. The Arctic Challenge was created and organized by Terje Haakonsen in 1999, in response to what he saw as too much interference from television and sponsors at snowboarding events. For over two hours, Shaun and the other competitors took turns doing runs on the unusually large halfpipe Haakonsen had created for the event. Judges did not announce scores until the end of the competition, so that the crowd could enjoy the aerial show with limited interruptions. "It didn't really seem like a contest," Shaun told a reporter. "It was really mellow, like riding with your friends—a jam session." He was having so much fun that he was still shredding (a slang term for snowboarding enthusiastically) when the judges announced the winner. "At the end, I heard some kids saying, 'Yeah, you won!' So I was stoked."[33]

Because the contest had limited sponsors, there was no prize money that year. But Shaun was thrilled nonetheless—especially since he had beaten Haakonsen, his childhood hero. Haakonsen

White relaxes at the 2001 Arctic Challenge in Norway, where he earned his first professional win.

himself presented him with two trophies: a gold one for first place in halfpipe and a silver one for overall best rider. "I got these two really sick trophies," Shaun said. "They look like Viking helmets. Terje's name was on the silver one because he won last year. Now my name's on it, and I'm invited back next year to try to hold the title. I'm not sure—I guess if I win three years in a row, I get to keep the trophy for good. That would be cool."[34]

Living It Up in Las Vegas

After doing one skateboarding demo with Tony Hawk in Salt Lake City, Utah, Shaun got to experience some of the perks that come with hanging out with rich and famous people. That night, Hawk took him on a spontaneous trip to the famous gambling city of Las Vegas, Nevada. A limousine picked them up at the airport and took them first to the Hard Rock Café for dinner, and then on to the famous Luxor Hotel. Shaun had never been in such an expensive and luxurious hotel before—he was especially fascinated by the television that rose out of a countertop at the push of a button. At fifteen, he was too young to gamble, so Hawk gave him a hundred dollars and sent him down to the hotel's huge video arcade. At the time it seemed like an enormous amount of money. He only managed to spend forty dollars of it and then treated himself to a huge ice cream cone.

"It Was Straight Out of *Mean Girls*"

After Shaun turned pro, getting his schoolwork done became a constant battle. "Think about being thirteen," he says, "in a hotel in Japan, and the lights are flashing and your friends are all, 'hey let's go out.' And you're trying to teach yourself algebra."[35] When he was travelling, which was much of the winter, he was unable to keep up with his assignments, and his grades plummeted. For instance, at the beginning of eighth grade, he was getting all A's and B's, but when he got back from a snowboarding trip, he was failing every subject. The school refused to give him credit for his experiences abroad—even for physical education.

Shaun also took time off from school to demonstrate his skateboarding skills. He rode for Tony Hawk's company, Birdhouse Skateboards. "I didn't have a sponsor in skating until I was about fifteen," he explains, "because I was like, 'You know what, I'm going to earn it. One day Tony's going to ask me to ride for

White poses with Tony Hawk, left, while riding a skateboard made by Hawk's company, Birdhouse Skateboards, in 2001.

Birdhouse.'"[36] When the offer came, Shaun was ecstatic. Tony, who had mentored Shaun for years, now thought he was good enough to represent his company.

It quickly got around school that Shaun had been sponsored by Tony Hawk's company. This made things even more difficult for him. People he thought were his friends suddenly wanted free snowboarding and skateboarding equipment. Others assumed he was stuck up and tried to take him down a peg or two. "It was straight out of *Mean Girls*," he remembers, comparing the experience to the 2004 film about high school cliques. "I'd be sitting in class and they'd be like, 'So, do you hang out with Tony Hawk ever?' I'd say 'Yeah, I hang out.' And then on my way out of the class, I'd hear that same kid say, "Shaun was just talking about hanging out with Tony Hawk all day.' If I talked about things that were normal in my life, it sounded like I was trying to impress somebody."[37]

His parents found a solution to Shaun's problems. The nearby town of Carlsbad had a special independent study program in its high school that allowed students in Shaun's position to work at their own pace. His parents took Shaun out of school in the middle of eighth grade, moved north to Carlsbad, and enrolled him in the program. Still, they were worried that Shaun would suffer socially from the change. Shaun was worried that he would be left behind academically. Neither happened. In fact, Shaun found he was learning more by combining his studies with his travel. For instance, while he was in Japan, he studied Japan, visiting Hiroshima (the city on which the United States had dropped an atomic bomb at the end of World War II) to gain perspective on the September 11, 2001, attacks on the United States. This gave Shaun real-world experience in subjects that his peers only learned about from books. "While all my classmates have the perception of 'that big tower in Paris,'" he said of the Eiffel Tower, "I can actually say, 'I stood on top of it!'"[38]

A Boy Among Men

Because Shaun took so much time off from school to snowboard, he had very few opportunities to hang out with people his own age. Most of his competitors were in their twenties, and Shaun had to learn how to socialize with adults. He also had to figure out how to have a little fun without breaking the law. This was not easy—at the time, snowboarders had a reputation for acting inappropriately. "Seeing all these guys getting drunk and coming home with random girls was super strange to me,"[39] Shaun remembers. He stayed away from the party lifestyle and concentrated on competing—and on his schoolwork. This made things a little lonely, but what was hardest on Shaun was not being able to attend the award ceremonies that were held in bars. Because

"I Just Kept Lying and Lying and Lying"

As a teenager, Shaun rarely lied to his parents. As long as he was honest with them, they usually supported anything he wanted to do. He remembers one notable exception, however. While on a small skateboarding tour with his brother Jesse, Shaun was part of a video shoot that required the riders to skate without their helmets and pads. This terrified his mother. "Every day she would call, and I was like, 'Yeah I'm wearing the helmet,' while I was dropping with nothing on, no pads, hitting my head and stuff," he remembers. "I just kept lying and lying and lying. And then Jesse gets on the phone and he says, 'He hasn't worn the helmet the whole time.' I was like, 'What are you doing?' He told on me!" Even though Jesse told their parents the truth, he did not try to stop Shaun from skating without protection. After all, assuming some risk was part of extreme sports. Still, Shaun remembers the fallout from his lie as being "pretty heavy."

Quoted in Method TV. "5 Minutes with Shaun White," March 22, 2007. www.youtube.com/watch?v=fjDt1p61dbg&list=PLE456C0A7F71C6AAF&index=2&feature=plpp_video.

Shaun was underage, he was not allowed inside—even if he had won the competition.

Eventually, his parents decided that he was old enough to be chaperoned by his older brother. Jesse took over as his tour manager, and traveled with Shaun all over the world. In hindsight, Jesse wondered whether this was a good idea: "I was 22 and just learning how to be an adult myself," he remembers. "It was way too much responsibility."[40] Jesse had to manage Shaun's travel, his interview schedule, and his endorsements and appearances. While he may have been overwhelmed by his new job at first, he quickly adapted, and Shaun loved having his older brother with him. With Jesse bridging the age gap between Shaun and the older snowboarders, Shaun could be more sociable. Their parents did not always approve of their sons' antics, such as the time they took part in a huge fire-extinguisher war in the hallway of a Japanese hotel. Still, it was a fun time for Shaun, and he remembers those early years fondly.

Around that time, Burton Snowboards offered Shaun an opportunity to design and endorse his own line of snowboarding equipment and clothing. Shaun agreed, on one condition. He did not want to work with Burton artists; he wanted Jesse, who had become a talented artist, to be his designer. Burton agreed and the two brothers teamed up, creating a wildly successful line together.

"Why Do I Need the Free Curly Fries?"

Spending so much time with adults had a positive side effect; it taught Shaun to be articulate and polite with the adults who interviewed him. He quickly gained a reputation for being a well-rounded kid able to handle fame well. And he was getting more and more famous. "I would reach these levels where people started asking for my autograph," he remembers. "All [of a] sudden my normal cursive signature wasn't good enough, you had to come up with something fancy."[41] He did more and more interviews, photo shoots, and appearances, getting comfortable with his growing fame. It helped that he had been in the spotlight since he was seven. "If it hadn't happened gradually," he said, "I wouldn't have been able to handle it."[42] However, he was still taken aback by the devotion of his fans. For instance, he once put a piece of ripped tee-shirt over his nose and mouth at an X-Games event because he forgot to bring sunscreen. "It was like this pirate thing," he said. "I was making aargghhh noises, being goofy."[43] Much to his surprise, kids all over the world began copying the look. Shaun had inadvertently started a fashion trend.

He also began earning bigger and bigger purses (prizes). One of his most memorable prizes was a car—which he was too young

White takes a break at a competition in 2001. Despite the fame and money that came to him at such a young age, he managed to stay grounded.

to drive—as well as fifty thousand dollars in cash. Shaun spread the cash out over the bed in his hotel room, marveling that he was looking at more money than his parents made in a year. After another win, he put thirty thousand dollars in cash into his carry-on luggage before returning home by plane, much to the surprise of the security guard who ran his bag through the X-ray machine.

While all that money would overwhelm most teenagers, Shaun never squandered it. Instead he bought his family a new house in Carlsbad and invested in several rental properties in the area. There was plenty of money left over for luxuries, however, such as the new Lexus IS 300 that he bought himself—even though he did not yet have a driver's license. "Tony [Hawk] bought a bunch of Lexuses, so I kind of got inspired and checked it out," he once told a reporter. "My sister is always snagging it when I'm gone."[44]

Along with the prize money and the fees he got for endorsing products, Shaun also got tons of freebies from his sponsors. His family and friends were happy to take the extra swag off his hands, and the rest piled up in the garage. By the time he was sixteen, he had sponsorship deals with Oakley sunglasses, T-Mobile, PlayStation, and Mountain Dew—and of course, Burton Snowboards, whom he had represented since he was seven years old. Shaun passed a lot of these gifts on. "It's cool just being able to share the perks with my friends and family," he said. "We all work hard at what we do, so it's a great treat to be able to hook up those around me."[45]

While Shaun was used to receiving free products from his sponsors, he still found it odd that the more money he made, the more people wanted to give him things for free. "I get absolutely bizarre, random stuff," he said. "Diamond necklaces and a yearly supply of Jamba Juice. Lasik eye surgery." The gifts made no sense to him. "Everyone knows I'm making a great living now," he said. "But it's funny, I'll go into a restaurant, and they'll say 'curly fries are on us.'" At the time, all he could think was, "'Dude, I walked past four [homeless people] on my way in here. Why do I need the free curly fries?'"[46]

The 2002 Olympics Qualifiers

In 2002, Shaun decided to try for a spot on the U.S. Olympic men's snowboarding team. Only four riders would make the team, based on their top two scores in five qualifying Grand Prix events. Going into the final event, Shaun's top two finishes were fourth and third, and he needed to win the fifth event to make the team. The judges had been watching Shaun closely that season, and most of them expected him to qualify. So did Peter Foley, head coach of the U.S. Olympic snowboarding team. "He's just naturally talented—insanely so,"[47] Foley told *USA Today*.

Before the final Grand Prix event, Shaun was philosophical about his chances. "If I make the Olympic team, that's cool," he said. "If I don't, that's cool, too. For me, snowboarding is just

White catches air during a halfpipe run at the 2002 U.S. Snowboard Grand Prix in Breckenridge, Colorado. He lost out on a chance to make the Olympic team in his final run.

about having fun."[48] Even though it seemed he was not focused on winning, he did very well. Riders are judged on maneuvers, rotations, amplitude, and overall style, and point values are averaged together to arrive at a final score. After the first of two runs, Shaun's average put him in the lead, and his spot on the team seemed like a sure thing. But in a startling upset in the final run, J.J. Thomas—who was not a favorite going into the competition—edged ahead of Shaun by a mere three-tenths of a point and won the final spot on the team.

Part of Something Bigger

The significance of his loss did not hit Shaun until a month later, when he watched the U.S. Olympic team sweep the men's halfpipe event on television. Ross Powers won the gold, Danny Kass won the silver, and J.J. Thomas won the bronze. In addition, American Kelly Clark won the gold in the women's halfpipe event. It was an emotional moment for America, coming less

Snowboarding Basics

Shaun White competes in four different types of snowboarding contests: halfpipe (including quarter-pipe), slopestyle, big air, and rail. Slopestyle is similar to riding through a snowboarding park—riders choose paths through terrain filled with jumps and obstacles, and they are judged on both difficulty and performance. Big air competitions feature a large artificial jump, and riders are scored on both the height of their jumps and the tricks that they perform while airborne. Rail contests feature a series of jibs (obstacles that a rider can jump or slide across), including rails, pipes,

White rides a rail on a slopestyle course in 2007.

and walls. White takes pride in thinking of himself as a snowboarder who can tackle whatever obstacle is put on the slope, and part of his success is due to this versatility.

Most snowboard and skateboard contests allow riders to do as many tricks as they can fit into their allotted time. In this respect, Shaun has an advantage—because he is so powerful, his speed allows him to fit an extra trick into his runs. He also jumps higher than his competitors, which gives him more time in the air to do more-complex tricks.

than a year after the September 11 terrorist attacks. Shaun realized then that the Olympics were not just another competition. They were about being part of something bigger, a team that represented one's country. Their outcome could affect the morale of an entire nation.

Shaun realized he had missed a great opportunity. For the first time, the boy who preferred to work alone wanted to be part of something larger than himself. Now he had a new goal: He vowed to represent the United States in the Olympics in 2006, and to win the gold. He would become the best professional snowboarder in the world. His competitive streak had never been stronger. Shaun White had gotten serious.

The Perfect Season

After his regrettable loss at the Olympic qualifiers, Shaun White's competitive drive kicked into high gear. Over the next four years, he won nearly every snowboarding contest he entered. He also took on a new challenge—he turned pro in skateboarding. By 2006, the nineteen-year-old had proved himself to be a top competitor in not one, but two sports. This time, he was going to the Olympics.

His Best Season Yet

Losing his spot on the Olympic team energized Shaun as never before. He closed out the 2002 season by taking first place in slopestyle at the World Snowboarding Championships and winning the Toyota Big Air event in Japan. The following season, he exceeded everyone's expectations by medaling in almost every event he entered. He swept both the Vans Triple Crown at Big Bear Mountain and The Session at Vail, taking first place in both halfpipe and slopestyle competitions at each event. He won a trip to Hawaii at the Kawasaki Triple Air event, and won the slopestyle contest at the U.S. Open—an event produced by his sponsor, Burton Snowboards. Shaun had never won a contest at the U.S. Open before, and the win was a milestone for him.

His most impressive accomplishment of the 2003 season was his outstanding performance at the winter X games. Shaun swept the snowboarding events, winning the gold in both the slopestyle and halfpipe competitions. In halfpipe, he beat all

White competes at the 2003 winter X Games in Aspen, Colorado, where he swept the snowboarding events.

four members of the 2002 Olympic snowboarding team. Ross Powers, who won the Olympic gold medal, came in second, and J.J. Thomas, who had edged Shaun out of a spot on the Olympic team by just three-tenths of a point, did not make it to the X Games podium. Shaun was named the X-Games "Best Athlete," a huge accomplishment for a sixteen-year-old who, according to popular wisdom, would not reach his peak until his mid-twenties.

Shaun closed out the 2003 season by taking first place at Terje Haakonsen's Arctic Challenge, this time in slopestyle. The half-pipe contest was canceled due to bad weather, much to the disappointment of the halfpipe riders, who had worked hard all year to qualify for the premier event. Despite the conditions, they decided to put on a show for the crowd and ride the halfpipe anyway. Shaun was awarded "Best Run" for his performance that day, and ended the 2003 season with more than ten first place awards. It was his best season yet.

"I Don't Belong Here"

With the winter over, Shaun again turned to skateboarding, as he did every summer. This season, however, he was thinking about pushing himself even further by turning pro. He talked it over with Hawk,

A Glossary of Skateboarding and Snowboarding Terms

Skateboarders and snowboarders use much of the same terminology, including:

540, 720, 1080, 1260: These numbers refer to the degrees the rider, or the board, spins. There are 360 degrees in a circle. Therefore, a 540 equals one and a half spins, a 1080 equals three spins, and so forth.

air: The altitude a rider achieves during a trick.

armadillo: A skateboarding trick of White's invention, it is actually a frontside heelflip 540 body varial. An incredibly difficult trick, the armadillo combines independent spins of both the rider and the skateboard.

backside: The opposite of *frontside*, this term refers to the direction the rider's feet face when he approaches a vert ramp or halfpipe wall to do a trick. If his heels face the ramp, he is performing the trick backside.

cab: Performing a mirror image of a frontside trick by leading with the weaker foot (riding switch) and spinning in the opposite direction.

cork: Short for "corkscrew," it refers to the diagonal motion of the rider's body when he spins and flips at the same time.

double cork: A class of snowboarding trick that combines two flips with multiple spins.

Continued next page

who told him to go for it. "I get paid a lot to snowboard, so it's my main sport," Shaun explained. "But I've always wanted to take some time off and skate. I'm having so much fun with it, so why not?"[49]

With less than a month to prepare, Shaun entered the Slam City Jam in Vancouver, Canada. Also known as the North American

double McTwist 1260: White's signature snowboarding trick, this maneuver combines two flips with three and a half spins.

fakie: Another term for *switch*.

frontside: The opposite of *backside*. If a rider's toes face the ramp as he begins a trick, he is performing it frontside.

goofy footed: In board sports, the stronger foot is placed on the back of the board. A goofy-footed rider prefers his left foot on the back.

grab: To grab the board with your hands. A common element in skateboarding tricks.

jib: Any obstacle or feature deliberately placed on a course.

McTwist: A trick consisting of a 540-degree rotation with a backflip. Named after its inventor, snowboarder Mike McGill.

regular footed: The opposite of *goofy footed*. A regular-footed rider is most comfortable with his right foot on the back of the board.

rodeo flip: Another name for an inverted frontside 540.

shred: To snowboard or skateboard enthusiastically or aggressively.

stalefish: A difficult grab trick in which the rider reaches behind his leg to grab the board. The awkward maneuver requires flexibility and plenty of air.

switch: To lead with the opposite foot; e.g., when a regular-footed rider rides switch, he rides goofy footed.

varial: Another name for a 180-degree rotation, or half spin. In skateboarding, the term can apply to either the rider or the board.

Skateboard Championships, Slam City is one of the preeminent skateboard contests in the world. "It was my first pro contest—so scary,"[50] he remembers. But he felt like it was something he had to do. He needed to be sure that turning pro in skating was right for him.

Though Shaun had been skateboarding since he was six years old, he felt awkward at the event. "I felt like I did years ago in snowboarding, like I just started," he remembers. "I could barely land my run and I didn't feel worthy enough to be on the ramp," he remembers. "I felt like, 'I don't belong here, I'm just winging it.'"[51] Despite his misgivings, he put on a spectacular performance, doing kickflips, frontside varial 540s, and even a 540 rodeo. He was so new to competitive skateboarding that he could not name many of the tricks he performed, but he still came in fourth, beating out world-famous skaters like Bucky Lasek and Pierre-Luc Gagnon. It was an amazing achievement for his first professional contest.

His performance at Slam City qualified him for a spot in the summer X Games. This upset some of the other pro skaters. Most of them had started in the amateur circuit, working their way slowly through the ranks. In their opinion, Shaun had not paid his dues. In addition, Shaun already had incredible financial success, and they saw his entry into skating as a threat to their livelihoods. "I'm facing what I got away from in snowboarding, like amateur contests," Shaun explains, remembering how parents of young snowboarders had complained that their kids did not have a chance when Shaun competed "I hate it—just seeing the petty side of skateboarding. . . . I showed up at a pro skate contest and a bunch of the vert skaters were like, 'What...is he doing here. I had to do the amateur contests, why doesn't he?'"[52]

Shaun came in sixth in vert at the 2003 summer X Games, but as his skating improved, he gradually gained the respect of his fellow skateboarders. But he still found it difficult to break into the social scene. This was frustrating, but it was nothing new—he also found it difficult to connect socially with other snowboarders. "Because I'm the guy that does both sports, I'm not really embedded in either," he explained. "Even the guys from snowboarding hang out all the time, after the season. But I disappear, I go skateboard and I don't really see a lot of those guys too much. . . . It's kind of like different parents. You're splitting the time and it's like, 'who really gets the most time?'"[53]

A Debilitating Injury

He continued to excel in both sports until the 2004 winter X Games, where he injured his right knee during his halfpipe qualifying run and had to sit out the finals. It turned out that he had torn the meniscus (cartilage) in his knee and had to have surgery to repair the damage. Hoping to still compete that season, he put too much strain on his injured knee after surgery and bruised the bone. He was forced to sit out the remainder of the 2004 season and endure six months of painful rehab. This was particularly frustrating because, for all his athletic abilities, the eighteen-year-old had never before lifted weights and had avoided the gym at all costs.

In 2005, he came back to snowboarding with a vengeance, again winning most of the contests he entered. When skateboarding season rolled around, he joined the Mountain Dew Tour, winning the vert skating contest at the first stop in Louisville, Kentucky. And at the summer X Games, he won his first silver

White grabs his board in mid-air at the summer X Games in 2005, where his silver-medal finish earned him respect in the skateboarding world.

medal in vert skating. He was no longer seen as an outsider in skateboarding. Stronger and faster after his knee rehab, he was now in the top tier of professional skateboarders.

An Undefeated Record

The first qualifier for the 2006 Olympic team was held in Breckenridge, Colorado—the same venue where he had been beaten out of a spot on the 2002 Olympic team when he was fifteen. Now nineteen, White was determined to make the team. He had worked hard that fall, training in New Zealand where winter was in full swing. And though he repeatedly told the media that the Olympics were just another snowboarding event—taking the same nonchalant attitude he had before the qualifiers in 2002—it was clear that the games meant a lot to him. In the previous four years, he had done everything he

White celebrates his first-place finish at the Chevrolet U.S. Snowboard Grand Prix in Vernon, New Jersey. Andy Finch, right, took second place; Steven Fisher, left, placed third.

could to prepare himself. He was determined not to miss his spot again.

That hard work paid off. White came in first in the halfpipe event at the Breckenridge Grand Prix. And then something remarkable happened. He won the second Grand Prix. And the third. And the fourth. He took a quick trip to Vail, Colorado, to compete in a rail jam competition, and he won that. Then he was off to Mountain Creek, New Jersey, for the fifth and final Grand Prix event. He won. The X Games were next, where he competed in both halfpipe and slopestyle. He took home double gold medals.

So far, it had been a perfect season. White was going to the Olympics with an undefeated record. Having won all five qualifiers, he was ranked first on the team. Now all he needed to do was bring home the gold.

Team USA

Immediately after the X Games, the USA snowboarding team left for Turin, Italy. The Olympic halfpipe competition was just six days away, and the team had a lot of work to do. White arrived pumped to compete, his goofy sense of humor in full force. Each time he was welcomed with the Italian greeting *buon giorno* ("good day"), he responded, "Hey, Bon Jovi!" According to *Rolling Stone*, "The locals would invariably correct him, so White would listen, nod, and then make them crazy by saying, 'Yeah, yeah, Bon Jovi.'"[54]

The Olympic Village seemed a bit disorganized to White. Some of the construction had not been finished, and the accommodations were not the best—there was a leak in White's bathroom, for example, that kept flooding his living area. On top of that, it could take hours to get through security at the training site. To get a jump on the day, Team USA got up before sunrise, venturing out in the freezing winter air and piling into the van that would take them to the mountain.

As he rode with his teammates each morning, he realized he did not have a lot of experience being part of a team—after all, he had avoided group activities his whole life, both in sports and in

White poses with snowboarding teammates Mason Aguirre, center, and Daniel Kass during the opening ceremony of the 2006 Winter Olympics.

school. Team USA did everything together—they dressed in the same uniforms, ate together, and traveled around the Olympic Village as a group. "You show up at the Olympics, and you're no longer you; you're an American Olympian," White explained. "You're part of this greater whole, and the individual doesn't matter."[55] In addition, his teammates snowboarded together year round, and some of them were good friends. White soon began to feel like an outsider. "There's a strange separation between me and the other guys,"[56] he remarked. But he did his best to share in the camaraderie.

The opening ceremonies were held on February 10, two days before the men's halfpipe competition. Until that point, White had forced himself to at least appear nonchalant, telling himself—and anyone who would listen—that the Olympics were no big deal. But when he marched in the opening ceremonies, waving the American flag overhead with his teammates, his calm gave way to awe. More than thirty thousand fans were crammed into the streets, cheering on the athletes. White had been in front of crowds before, but nothing compared with this.

A Devastating Fall

The halfpipe competition was held two days later. Even though Olympic snowboard teams are made of up of some of the best athletes in the world, each member still has to make at least one qualifying run. The twelve riders with the highest scores—the top six in each of two qualifying runs—advance to the finals and compete for the gold. Even though White was favored to win the gold, he did not take the qualifying rounds lightly. Anything can happen on any given day in the halfpipe.

Because of his high ranking, White ran first. He stood at the top of the slope that descended into the halfpipe in his Team USA uniform, an American flag bandana covering his nose and mouth. There were thousands of spectators surrounding the pipe, and though many of them were Italian, they cheered loudest for White. He took it all in, marked the spot where his family sat, and then rode down the slope and dropped into the pipe.

He knew right away that something was wrong. The enormity of the event had broken his concentration. He tried to find his "zone"—the mental place where muscle memory took over—and then the unthinkable happened. He came out of a spin, touched down on the snow—and fell.

White did not realize the magnitude of his mistake until he came out of the pipe and saw the look on his brother's face. The stumble had cost him; his score was a disappointing 37.7 out of a possible 50 points. The rest of his team scored in the 43 point range and would advance to the finals, but White dropped into seventh place and would have to take another qualifying run. If that was not bad enough, the run order was reversed on the second qualifier, and he would have to go last. That meant he had to wait two full hours for his turn—an eternity for a perfectionist whose instinct was to jump back up and repeat the run immediately.

"It's Like He Was Skating"

His coach, Bud Keene, immediately went to work, trying to get White into the right frame of mind. Keene told ESPN:

> He was rattled. I suggested that we take some runs to stay loose, but at first he declined. As I watched him stand and stare into the pipe at the top, and saw smoke coming out of his ears, I got more aggressive about my suggestion. He finally relented, and we went freeriding, taking six or seven runs until it was almost time for him to go. We rode the chairlift together, and talked openly about the situation, and I did what I do naturally to get him into a frame of mind to win. We pulled up to the top of the pipe after our last free-run, and with about 10 minutes to spare, handed his board to our wax tech to get buffed out.[57]

White makes his first run in the halfpipe finals at the 2006 Olympics. His seemingly effortless performance earned him the gold medal.

Moments later, White was standing in the staging area, calm and determined. As he started down the slope, AC/DC's song "Back in Black," blared over the sound system. It was the song White had trained to all year. He dropped into the pipe, and everything fell into place. The crowd seemed to disappear. As he spun through the air, he closed his eyes, letting his body take over. Less than a minute later, he was out of the pipe and waiting anxiously for his score. It was the highest in the field, moving him into the number one position once again. White had made it to the finals.

He was scheduled to run in the middle of the pack, so he had some time to prepare himself for the moment to come. All of a sudden, his nose started to bleed—the cold, dry mountain air had irritated his nasal passages. As he frantically tried to keep the blood off his American flag bandana, a camera crew rushed him, intent on getting footage of his bloody nose. He avoided them, stopped the bleeding, and composed himself once again.

As his name was announced for his run, White stepped onto the slope and pumped his arms into the air, raising a deafening cheer from the crowd. Then he dropped into the pipe—and into the zone. Even though style is not a factor in scoring the Olympic halfpipe contest, his run appeared to be effortless. He fit six tricks into his allotted time, each more complicated and elaborate than the last. His landings were fluid and controlled, as if he were floating back to earth. "It's like he was skating,"[58] Keene later told the *New York Times*.

His run earned an amazing 46.8 points. He was solidly in first place. And as the last rider came out of the pipe, it became official. Shaun White had won the gold.

The Best Part of Any Win

Immediately after his run, White was wrapped in an American flag and escorted to the podium along with his teammate Danny Kass, who had won the silver. An Olympic gold medal—a disc weighing over half a pound—was placed around his neck. From up on the platform, he spotted his family standing together

White holds the American flag while celebrating his gold-medal win in the halfpipe event at the 2006 Olympics.

in the crowd, and the enormity of the moment overwhelmed him. "It hit me when I saw my whole family in tears," he said. "I got all choked up thinking about what it meant to them after the years of driving me to competitions, sleeping in a van, and what they had to give up. And what it meant to just be getting a gold medal in a sport people thought was crazy. It was life-changing for me."[59]

When the ceremony was over, everyone rushed the podium. His sister, Kari, waved frantically to him—she was stuck behind a barricade and could not get past the traffic jam of people. White yelled, "Kari! Just jump!"[60] and Kari, who had been the U.S. Open junior halfpipe champion in 2000, leapt over the barricade and ran into her little brother's arms. Soon the whole family was reunited, and all of White's usual cool and composure was replaced by unabashed elation. As he would tell television host Oprah Winfrey a few years later, the best part of any win is the big family hug that awaited him at the bottom of the mountain.

Chapter 4

The Price of Fame

Alfter winning the Olympic gold medal in 2006, Shaun White was world famous. It took some time for him to adjust to both the upside and downside of instant fame, but he never lost sight of what made him truly happy: competition. He decided he would see whether he could again rise to the top—this time in skateboarding.

The Flying Tomato

As soon as White won Olympic gold, his life changed forever. He got the first hint of this on the flight home; all of the flight attendants immediately recognized him and asked to see his gold medal. Later, as he walked through the airport in New York, people spotted his long red hair and burst into spontaneous applause. He went to a Knicks game the next night, and when the cameras caught him on the JumboTron, the whole of Madison Square Garden stood up and applauded. "It was unbelievable," White said. "I sat down, and I was shaking."[61]

Tony Hawk had given White the nickname "The Flying Tomato" years ago, because of the way White's red hair swept behind him when he flew by on a skateboard. Now, much to White's embarrassment, the whole world was calling him that. The nickname even prompted an endorsement offer from Heinz ketchup. White politely refused.

More endorsement offers poured in. Quite a few of them played on the California board-athlete stereotype of a lazy, dumb sort of beach bum. White rejected those, regardless of how much

White poses with his gold medal during an appearance on MTV's Total Request Live in February 2006. His Olympic success made him an instant celebrity.

money he was offered. "I thought that would be so terrible, if I had done well and then right away I'm in some commercial saying 'dude' and 'awesome,' and 'hey bro,'" he explained. "It would have just made everybody look dumb."[62] He realized that he was fast becoming the loudest voice in snowboarding, and he felt a responsibility to portray the sport professionally. He chose his endorsements very carefully, talking each one through with Jesse and his management team.

He also chose his words carefully. In interviews, he did his best not to slip into California slang and rider jargon. He wanted to do everything he could to show the world that snowboarding was a legitimate sport populated by serious athletes. "The biggest compliment I've ever gotten," he said, "was after the Olympics. A friend of mine came up to me and said 'Hey man, thanks for keeping us looking solid in the media.' . . . I thought that was cool, to have respect from guys within the sport."[63]

Why All the Freebies?

The companies that sponsor sports stars usually do so because they want to pair their product with a strong, athletic image. They give athletes free products in the hope that their merchandise will get media exposure and buzz. For instance, one of Shaun White's sponsors, Mountain Dew, once gave him a free vending machine. White showed off the vending machine during several interviews, making sure the company's product got exposure. In return, White's friends got free soda whenever they stopped by.

White has had sponsors since he was seven years old. He was so used to receiving free clothing that he never had to shop for himself. Once he got older and became interested in fashion, he had to get used to the idea of trying clothes on in a store. "The concept of a dressing room just blew my mind," he said. "I was like, 'You're going to let me put on these pants, right here?'"

Quoted in Vanessa Grigoriadis. "Up in the Air." *Rolling Stone*, March 18, 2010.

Even though he understood that his fame came with responsibilities, he still had fun with it. When the City of San Diego offered to throw him a parade, he joked that he would require a diamond-encrusted goblet to carry on his float. He loved telling the story about how his mother took his gold medal to the dry cleaners after he got a food stain on the ribbon. He was invited to celebrity parties. His face was on the cover of major magazines. Wherever he went, he was congratulated. His long mop of red hair made him instantly recognizable.

But it was still snowboarding season, and the U.S. Open was a few weeks away. White stepped away from his celebrity and prepared for the competition. He had ten first place wins under his belt, but that was not good enough. He wanted a perfect season.

So he made it happen. At the U.S. Open in March, he took first in both the halfpipe and the slopestyle events. He later told *Rolling Stone*, "I like the idea that you can do whatever you want to do. That's what life is about."[64]

The Nineteen-Year-Old Millionaire

After the post-Olympics frenzy settled down, White returned to his family home in Carlsbad. He wanted to celebrate with his friends, but they had graduated high school the year before and were all working nine-to-five jobs or away at college. With no one but his mom to hang out with all day, he quickly grew restless. So he did what any nineteen-year-old millionaire would do after winning the Olympic gold—he bought a house of his own.

It was a seven-bedroom mansion set on several acres in nearby Rancho Santa Fe—one of the most affluent communities in the country. His neighbors were older and well established, and they assumed the skinny kid with all the boxes would soon be joined by his parents. When they realized who he was, they were welcoming enough, but it was clear that he would have a hard time fitting into the neighborhood.

He also discovered that being a homeowner meant dealing with one headache after another, and soon he hated the house. In addition, living alone was not all it was cracked up to be. He had never bought groceries before, and trips to the store were daunting—especially since he could not leave his house without being recognized. On one occasion, a group of kids followed him around the grocery store for hours, whispering to each other about every item he chose. White joked about it in an interview: "'Ah, he's getting the non-fat yogurt, he must be on a diet!'"[65] he imagined them saying.

It was not long before he felt trapped in the huge, rambling house. So he did what had always fulfilled him in the past—he threw himself back into snowboarding. The 2007 season was about to start. This year, he would take it easy and just have fun. At least, that was his plan.

White soars through the air during a practice at the 2007 winter X Games in Aspen, Colorado, during a season that proved to be a letdown from his success the previous year.

As it turned out, just having fun was far more difficult than he expected. His travel schedule was grueling; he was doing dozens of endorsements, making a film about his life, and competing all over the world—all at the same time. His focus was shot, and his snowboarding suffered for it. A camera crew traveled with him, documenting his season, which included a lackluster performance at the winter X Games (he came in second in halfpipe and third in slopestyle). "I'm torn in all these different directions," he complained. "I'll be so worked about everything else that I'm not even focusing on the contest."[66] He closed out the season feeling disjointed, like he had lost his footing. What he needed was a new goal. Nothing made him happier than a challenge.

Could He Do It Again?

As the 2007 skateboarding season approached, White set his sights on the vert competition at the summer X Games. A gold medal in vert skating would prove to everyone in the skating community that he was more than just a snowboarder fooling around on a skateboard. It also would give him a chance to recapture the joy of his first big win so many years ago. As he explained in *Don't Look Down*, a documentary about him:

> Winning the X games in skateboarding would mean so much to me. Because it's the first time, all over again. It's like the first time you ever won a big contest. You can't get that feeling back. But for me to do that in skating would be that for sure. It would go on the wall right next to the Olympic medal.[67]

White threw himself into practice, training hard on Tony Hawk's vert ramp in Carlsbad. When asked why White was suddenly pushing himself so hard—especially after his phenomenal year in snowboarding in 2006—Hawk said:

> I think the key to having success like Shaun is that he has the highest expectations of himself. There are certain guys that reach that level and they lose their motivation. They're like,

The Basics of Skateboarding

Almost all skateboarding tricks are based on these three basic moves:

The Ollie: Anyone who has watched someone skateboarding has probably seen an ollie. The rider jumps and the skateboard jumps with him, appearing to adhere to his feet until he lands. The secret to the ollie is to step hard on the back of the skateboard while jumping upwards, literally bouncing it off the ground. While airborne, the feet control the board, leveling it out flat before the landing.

The Kickflip: The rider performs an ollie. While rider and board are airborne, the rider flips the board a full 360 degrees under his feet, as if he is flipping a coin.

The Shuvit: The rider jumps and, with his feet, spins the board 180 degrees.

I'm number one, I'm over it. And then, that's it. Everyone forgets about them. But when you have a mentality like Shaun's, you get to that stage and you're like, what's next? What else can I do? How hard can I push this? It doesn't matter that he's won everything. For Shaun, to win the X Games would be his coming of age in skating. That's it—he's the best vert skater. There you go.[68]

"I Couldn't Let Myself Fall"

His first competition of the season was on the Dew Tour, a multisport event that made five stops across the United States. At the end of the tour, the highest-ranked competitor in each sport was awarded the coveted Dew Cup. White had never won a Dew Cup before, and he wanted one this year. His biggest competitors were Bucky Lasek and Pierre-Luc Gagnon—both legends in the skate community and at the top of their game. They both skated for Birdhouse, and White knew them well. But he did not think they viewed him as enough of a threat on the ramp. He planned to change that.

On the first stop of the tour, he took first place with a score of 94.25—the highest vert score in the tour's history. He won the second event as well, and the third, pulling out a varial frontside 540—a trick that only White can execute in competition. One of his strengths is his ability to spin better than anyone else, something he hoped his competitors would now recognize and respect. "I got in there and kind of mixed things up so at least they look at me differently when I go on the ramp—like a guy who's going to land a good run," he explained. "I don't know if I was having that effect before. I feel it in snow, where there's the expectation that I'll do well, but not as much in skating because I haven't had a spree like I'm going on now."[69]

Finally, it was time for the big event, the summer X Games. Both Lasek and Gagnon had stayed right on White's heels on the Dew Tour, but with three wins under his belt, White had momentum. Still, Gagnon was a two-time gold medalist in vert, and either he or Lasek could easily take the contest.

Since falls are so common in skateboarding, most vert competitions allow skaters three runs, counting only the highest score. White and Gagnon both fell on their first run, but Gagnon nailed his second, pulling into first place. Tony Hawk was a commentator at the event and claimed Gagnon pulled off the lowest 720 degree spin he had ever seen, spinning just a few feet above the lip of the ramp.

On his second run, White tried to take Gagnon, but again he fell, dropping to sixth place. As one of the commentators pointed out, White was now under tremendous pressure—he only had one more chance to catch Gagnon and take the gold. "That's the way he likes it, I'm telling you," Hawk said. "That's what he needs."[70]

White's third run was outstanding. He pulled off a huge McTwist, easily made his 720, and did a slick stalefish frontside rodeo. When his score was announced—a 95.75 out of a possible 100 points—he threw his helmet in celebration so hard that

White competes at the 2007 summer X Games, where an exceptional final run earned him a dramatic come-from-behind victory.

White celebrates his win at the Dew Tour stop in Baltimore, Maryland, in June 2007, the year he won the Dew Cup.

he knocked the padding out of it. He had beaten Gagnon, and had won the top vert skateboarding competition on the planet. "This means the world to me," he said afterwards. "Pierre threw down the gauntlet for me, you know? . . . It just came together. I couldn't let myself fall."[71]

Coming of Age in Skating

His winning streak ended on the fourth Dew Tour stop, and on the fifth, Bucky Lasek scored a 95.5, beating White's record of 94.25 and winning the contest. Still, with three wins out of five, White was awarded the Dew Cup. With his X Games and Dew Tour wins, he had shown the skate community that he was not only on par with the other top tier skaters, he was arguably the best vert skater in the world. They would never look at him in the same way again.

Chapter 5

Project X

After winning the X-Games gold medal in vert skateboarding, Shaun White turned his attention back to snowboarding. The 2010 Olympics were just a few short years away. He began to think about what it would take to again win the gold. One thing was clear—he had gone as far as he could with the tricks in his repertoire. It was time to push the sport forward.

A Dangerous Maneuver

In 2006, White had won the Olympic gold medal by showcasing his 1080 spins and his signature trick, the McTwist—a backflip combined with a 540 degree spin. Combining a flip and a spin is called a cork maneuver, named after the corkscrewing motion of the rider, who flips off-axis, on the diagonal. It was one of the most difficult tricks in snowboarding, and White had to figure out how to surpass it. The natural next step was to add more flips and spins to the McTwist.

White had a list of double cork maneuvers that he had always wanted to try, including the frontside double cork 1080—two end-over-end flips combined with three complete rotations. The problem was that double cork maneuvers were extremely dangerous. No one had figured out how to do them because they were so hard to practice safely. "When you're coming down into the pipe, you're flipping forward, looking at the lip of the pipe," White explains. "Your head is ducking right past it. So the level of danger with it is really high."[72]

White makes his slopestyle run at the 2008 European Open in Switzerland. He won the event but placed second in the halfpipe despite the addition of a new trick, the McTwist 1260.

At the 2008 European Open, it became clear that White would have to learn the double cork if he wanted to remain at the top of his sport. He executed his run perfectly, and even threw in a brand new trick, the McTwist 1260. But in an exciting upset, he was beaten by Kevin Pearce, a rising star who had recently added back-to-back 1080s to his run. "Shaun's never been in a position where he does the perfect run and doesn't win," Pearce said after the competition. "That was the first time. Now I know I can beat him. And he knows it too."[73]

The Secret Halfpipe

That summer, White discussed ways to prepare for the 2010 Olympics with his sponsors from Red Bull. He needed a way to develop double cork maneuvers safely and in private. Red Bull suggested building a halfpipe in a remote location, complete with a foam pit that would allow White to land the double cork safely. To keep the pipe private, they had to choose a site deep in the backcountry, accessible only by snowmobile or helicopter. Logistically, building such a structure would be a nightmare. But Red Bull was committed to seeing White win the gold in 2010, and they took on the challenge.

Construction began in late 2008, at a privately owned site in the San Juan Mountains just outside of Silverton, Colorado. The construction team was made up of some of the best engineers and halfpipe cutters in the business. Halfpipe cutting is tricky—a pipe can look perfect, but if the snow isn't packed and shaped correctly, it can be difficult to ride. Most pipes are cut from artificially made snow, which is not consistent throughout; these pipes usually have icy patches, which can be difficult for a snowboarder to maneuver. Red Bull's team wanted to cut White's halfpipe out of natural snow, which is consistently firm and dry all the way through. However, they needed a snow depth of at least thirty feet in order to cut the pipe. To accomplish this, they dropped explosive charges from a helicopter onto the mountainside. This created a series of avalanches which flooded the valley below.

Next, three specially designed snow cats equipped with curved cutting extensions, called Pipe Dragons, scooped out a 500-foot halfpipe (152.4m) with 22-foot high walls (6.7m), modeled after the halfpipe used in the X Games. At the same time, a 20- x 30-foot steel box (6.1 x 9.1m) that would become the foam pit was constructed from more than 4 tons (3.6t) of steel. It was

"I Think It Chose Me"

Shaun White seems to have been born for board sports. When asked why he chose to focus on the snowboard and skateboard, he explained, "I don't really think I chose it, I think it chose me. . . . I was six years old when I started, and I was sponsored at seven. I don't know that I had much of a choice."[1] He also believes that what you grow up with determines what sport you focus on and the type of athlete you become. He knows snowboarders from Norway who grew up skiing down huge mountains, and he acknowledges that they know how to navigate that type of terrain far better than he ever will. "It just breeds different styles," he explains. "That's why I skate vert instead of street. Everybody grows up different."[2]

[1] Quoted in Larry King Live. CNN, February 22, 2010. www.youtube.com/watch?v=0VoMWO-jrjY.
[2] Quoted in Sportskool. "One on One with Shaun White." HBO, 2008. Streamed online via Grace Creek Media. www.sportskool.com/sports/snowboarding.

assembled 7 miles (11.2km) away from the site and placed on skids, which are used to slide something along the ground. The team had to wait for a snowstorm to cover the road with snow so they could slide the structure along the road. It took a dump truck and several snow cats to get it up the road and over the mountain.

This was not the first time a foam pit had been placed at the end of a halfpipe so that a snowboarder could land a difficult trick safely; however, it was the first time anyone had ever constructed a halfpipe complete with foam pit in the backcountry. When White flew in by helicopter and saw it for the first time, he was stunned. "It looked like a field of flowers with a tank in the middle of it. It just didn't belong [there]," he said. "It was just some weird contrast, this godly halfpipe nestled in the middle of these mountains. . . . It was out of a freaking movie."[74]

Nailing the Double Cork

White started practice in February 2009, and not a moment too soon. Less than a month before, Kevin Pearce had beaten White in the European Open for the second year in a row. And while White won the gold in the X Games halfpipe event that season,

White's first-place halfpipe routine at the Snowboarding World Cup in Cardrona, New Zealand, in August 2009 saw the debut of his double cork tricks.

Pearce's run was superb. Many in the snowboarding community believed that Pearce should have won, and they began to rally behind Pearce—in part because they were tired of White being the sole face of snowboarding. It seemed unfair that, in a sport with so many talented riders, only one was offered multimillion dollar endorsements. As Pearce told the *New York Times*, "I feel the last couple years, Shaun has kind of dominated snowboarding. I think that people are getting sick of it, and they're getting sick of seeing him."[75]

At the secret halfpipe site in Silverton, dubbed "Project X" by Red Bull, White learned the frontside double cork 1080 in a single day. He figured out the trick by going back and forth between the foam pit and the pipe wall, practicing each element of the trick separately. By the end of that first day, he had it down and landed it in the pipe. "Just today, we've probably gotten in at least a couple of years of riding," White said. "I say that because, you have to have that perfect day, where the snow's just right, you're feeling strong, and you've got the picture of the trick you want to do in your head."[76] White was doing something that no one had ever done before. His work at Silverton proved that a rider can invent a trick, practice it in the foam pit, and then quickly bring it to realization on the halfpipe in a matter of hours.

The foam pit did not eliminate the danger, however. It was filled with softball-sized foam blocks that, according to White, "pushed back,"[77] and it was easy to sustain an injury. A few days into practice, White did just that, tearing a ligament in his thumb that required emergency surgery. But he was not done with the double cork 1080 yet. While he was in the hospital, the team moved the foam pit to the other end of the pipe so that White could learn a mirror image of the trick, known as a "cab" maneuver. To do the trick cab, he would have to approach the wall "fakie," or with his weaker foot on the back of the board, and then execute the spin in the opposite direction. This caused additional problems with the physics of the trick. He had to work out how much momentum he needed, when to spin and tuck his body, how to orient himself for the landing, and so forth. In the upcoming days, he nailed the cab double cork 1080, as well as a host of other double cork tricks, including the double McTwist 1260—two flips and three and a half spins.

When spring hit Colorado and the snow began to melt, White went to Mount Hood in Oregon to work on putting together a run made up of his new tricks. In August, he unveiled his double cork tricks at the Snowboarding World Cup in Cardrona, New Zealand. He easily took first place, stunning the crowd with his dizzying acrobatics above the pipe.

"It's Something You Don't Want To Hear"

Snowboarders are a tight-knit group, and White knew that other riders had been working on double cork maneuvers as well. In December, at the first Olympic Grand Prix, Louie Vito performed several spectacular double corks on his final run, taking second place to White's first. Kevin Pearce fell during the competition, but he was confident that in a few more weeks he would have the double cork nailed and would make the Olympic team. The media began to frame the Olympics as a head-to-head battle between White and Pearce. Though the two snowboarders sometimes criticized each other in the press, they were friends, and they both enjoyed the way the media was playing up their rivalry.

On New Year's Eve, 2009, Pearce was practicing his double corks in Park City, Utah, in preparation for the second Grand Prix event. As he attempted to land the dangerous trick, his body over-rotated and he struck his face on the lip of the half-pipe. He was rushed to the hospital, where it was determined that he had fractured his eye socket and that blood was leaking into his brain. Pearce had suffered eye damage as well as a devastating traumatic brain injury. He would never compete on the halfpipe again.

News of Pearce's injury struck the snowboarding community hard. White was shocked when he heard of the accident. "When I learned how serious it was, I was blown away," White remembers. "I didn't know how to feel with something like

An elated White raises his snowboard in victory after his third consecutive win at the winter X Games in Aspen, Colorado, in 2010.

that happening so close to home. It's something you don't want to hear or believe."[78] The tragedy provoked discussion in the media about the danger of the new double cork maneuvers, but no changes were made to competition rules. The general consensus among event organizers was that snowboarding was an extreme sport and, as such, was inherently dangerous. As long as riders understood the risks and took adequate precautions, they were free to explore the boundaries of the sport as they saw fit.

Pearce's friends distributed "I Ride For Kevin" stickers at the second Grand Prix, and nearly all of the snowboarders, including White, displayed them on their equipment. That day, White was beaten by Danny Davis, who had also perfected double cork maneuvers and had put together a spectacular run. Davis was thought to be a shoe-in for the Olympic team, but he injured his back in a snowmobile accident and had to drop out of the competition. At the end of the Grand Prix series, White again ranked first, earning him the top spot on the Olympic team. Louie Vito, Scotty Lago, and Greg Bretz made the team as well.

Then it was on to the winter X Games. White still was having trouble with the double McTwist 1260, and in a practice session before the contest, he missed his landing and smashed the side of his head against the lip of the halfpipe. He hit the ice so hard he knocked his helmet off. But he was lucky; unlike Pearce, he walked away with just a bruise on his jaw. He was dazed, but got back in the pipe and continued with practice. "If I backed out at that point, and saved myself for the Olympics," he explained, "I just feel like it would have mentally messed me up. I ran immediately back up to the top, furious, dropped back in, and did it again."[79]

His perseverance paid off; he nailed the trick in competition, blowing the crowd away with a run that also included a 23-foot air (7m) and back-to-back double cork 1080s. White won the gold with a score of 95.33, making it a three-peat: his third consecutive win at the winter X Games. Two weeks later, he headed to Vancouver, Canada, to see whether he could once again bring home the Olympic gold.

It's Lonely at the Top

There is a notion among top athletes that in order to be great, a competitor must be totally focused on winning—even at the expense of friendships. Kevin Pearce put this notion to the test by forming "Frends," a group of snowboarders dedicated to cheering each other on in competition. "People think that to be Kelly Slater or Tiger [Woods] or Shaun [White], you have to be a certain type of person," Pearce said. "I think it would be cool to see someone change that idea."[1] The group calls itself "Frends" because there is no "I" in friendship, and it has since formed an online business together.

Shaun White (who is not part of Frends) has a different view of competition and friendship, however. "I don't think you can have really good friends that you go and compete with, and when you beat them . . . you're buddy-buddy when you get down from the hill," he told Bob Simon of *60 Minutes*. "If you and I were competing on the hill, I don't think I'd want to hang out with you afterward while you're shining your medal. That would be a bummer."[2]

[1] Quoted in Alyssa Roenigk. "This Is Not Shaun White." *ESPN: The Magazine*, January 15, 2009. http://espn.go.com/action/news/story?id=3830833.
[2] Quoted in *60 Minutes*. "White: It's Sometimes Lonely at the Top." CBS News. July 12, 2010. www.cbsnews.com/2100-18560_162-6151366.html.

"Just Unreal"

Because he had spent so little time in Turin, Italy, the 2006 Olympics were just a blur in White's memory. This time, he decided to make an effort to enjoy the experience and socialize more with his teammates. "I didn't really know what that meant to be on the U.S. Team," he later admitted. "Obviously, I competed in Torino [Turin], but I . . . didn't get the chance to take in the whole vibe down in the city and do everything. This time around was just unreal. I was proud to run around with the U.S.A. gear on and do the whole [Olympic] thing."[80] He spent time with other

G BRETZ   LOUIS VITO   SHAU

www.olympic.org   ooo   vancouver 2010   ooo   www.olympic

*White, left, appears with members of the U.S. Olympic
snowboard halfpipe team, including Gregory Bretz, Louie
Vito, Scott Lago, Hannah Teter, Gretchen Bleiler, Kelly
Clark, and Elena Hight, at a press event before the start of
competition in February 2010.*

athletes in the Olympic Village, enjoyed Vancouver, and cheered
on other athletes alongside his teammates.

Still, his relationship with his teammates was more competitive than friendly, in part because White was too preoccupied
about the upcoming competition to be as sociable as he would
have liked. His teammates did not go out of their way to ease his
mind; each morning in the van, Louie Vito would beat him to
the shotgun seat so that he could use the stereo to try to throw
White off his game. "He'd play stuff he knew I hated, like Miley
Cyrus' 'Party in the U.S.A,' which is just painful," White said. "It's
bumming me out even thinking about it."[81]

Ever since he had started working on the dangerous double cork
maneuvers, White had been on edge. He was especially concerned

about landing the double McTwist 1260, which he still did not have down. His coach recognized this, so on the day before the contest—while everyone else was frantically practicing their runs—Keene took him on a kayaking trip in Horseshoe Bay. It turned out to be just what he needed. White spent a fun-filled day on the water with family and friends, relaxing and recharging his batteries. He was not above taking a few chances in the boat, however. "I had to be the guy who stood up on the kayak, obviously, and tried to pet the giant seal that came by to hang,"[82] he said.

"I Willed Myself to Land It"

On the day of the contest, White was still nervous about his qualifying run, even though it did not include the double McTwist 1260. Despite his worries, he nailed the run and went into the

White holds the end of his snowboard during a halfpipe run at the 2010 Winter Olympics. He landed the double McTwist 1260 and won the gold medal.

finals in first place. He was scheduled to go last in the finals, and as he watched the eleven other riders drop into the pipe, he was still trying to decide whether he would do the double McTwist. He had been talking about it to the press for months, and everyone in the stands expected it. But he still was not landing it consistently in practice. After changing his mind a dozen times, he finally decided to get it out of the way and attempt it on his first run in the finals.

And then, right before dropping into the pipe, he changed his mind again, and did the run without it.

Even without the double McTwist, White scored a 46.8 out of a possible 50 points, putting him in the lead. And in the lead he stayed. As the second round of final runs played out, no one could beat his score. White had won the gold. There was no need to do a second run at all.

But this was the Olympics, and the double McTwist had haunted him all season. He decided he was going to take a second run and try it. When his coach realized what White was going to do, he took him aside and warned him that if he was going to do the trick, he needed to be fully committed. Keene knew that White sometimes missed his landings if the pressure was not on. But White had worked on the trick for so long that he was not going to let himself miss the landing at the Olympics. "I willed myself to land it,"[83] he said.

And he did. His victory run was dazzling; ESPN described it as "the most explosive, exciting 30 seconds of riding all night." After the preliminary awards ceremony, White said, "I think about how many times I have done that run in my mind, and to land it here feels incredible. Now I can go to sleep."[84]

Beyond the Olympics

With more than a dozen X Games medals and two Olympic wins under his belt, there was not much left for White to accomplish. But he never considered slowing down. In the summer of 2010, he went undefeated in vert skating on the Dew Tour, again winning the Dew Cup in skateboarding. In 2011 he won his second gold

White flies above the crowd at the winter X Games in 2011, where he won his fourth gold medal in as many years; he also won the event in 2012.

medal in vert skating at the summer X Games. And in snowboarding, he won his fifth-straight halfpipe competition at the 2012 winter X Games, winning the gold with the first-ever perfect score in X Games history.

As of September 2012, White was twenty-six years old. He was at the peak of his powers as a professional snowboarder and skateboarder, and he had earned his place in history alongside board-sport legends like Tony Hawk and Terje Haakonsen. Having won every major snowboarding and skateboarding competition on the planet, all White needs now is another contest to conquer.

Chapter 6

What Makes Him Tick?

What does it take to be a top athlete like Shaun White? Natural ability is key, but it is not the whole story. As his coach, Bud Keene, points out, "His bone, body, brain and synapses make him who he is, but talent is not a rare commodity among professional athletes."[85] To reach White's level of achievement, it takes a rare combination of desire, an obsession with perfection, and a fierce competitive spirit. There is also a downside to having these innate characteristics, however; they can make life outside of the competitive arena difficult. As both an elite athlete and as a young man trying to navigate the strange world of sports stardom, White shares these challenges with many other young athletes at the top of their sport.

"He Works Harder than Anyone"

Keene believes the key to White's phenomenal success is his obsession with practice. "What sets him apart is his extreme commitment to training, to perfection," Keene says. "He has an uncompromising attitude toward his efforts. He works harder than anyone, and he's the most talented. That's a hell of a package."[86]

Even though he is obsessed with practice, White has to avoid pushing himself to exhaustion to avoid overtaxing his heart. But because snowboarding and skateboarding are not endurance sports, he does not need to do extreme cardiovascular training.

White tracks crisscross the snow during a practice session in Breckenridge, Colorado, in 2005. His commitment to practice allows him to gain the muscle memory needed to make his runs look effortless.

In fact, board sport athletes have a reputation for rarely working out in the gym. Until his knee injury in 2004, which required months of intense physical therapy, White was no exception. In practice, he focuses on honing muscle memory, repeating his maneuvers over and over until they are second nature. White will not perform a trick in public until he can make it look easy. His effortless style has set him apart from many other talented riders, and is one of the things that makes him so much fun to watch.

"I Just Feel It"

For muscle memory to kick in, an athlete has to have enough confidence in himself that he can trust his body to take over. White has good reason to have faith in his abilities, but his confidence

Constantly Competitive

For all of his hard work and confidence, one of the strongest factors in Shaun White's success is his fierce competitive drive. Unfortunately, that competitiveness extends into every area of his life. There is no such thing as a friendly game. Even when he is just playing cards with his family, it drives him crazy to lose.

When asked to describe his competitive nature, White gave an example of a time he was playing a board game with his family after a competition. "I had won the X Games, and then I lost a game of Monopoly, and it was like the end of the world. Even though I had just conquered this huge thing, I can lose a card game or something and I'm just so bitter."

Quoted in Sportskool. "One on One with Shaun White." HBO, 2008. Streamed online via Grace Creek Media. www.sportskool.com/sports/snowboarding.

goes deeper than that. "I already feel, when I walk out on the snow, that I have an advantage," he explains. "I always feel that, just in my head. . . . It's not that I know [that I am going to win], I just feel it."[87] White assumes he will win—and because he believes it, he usually does.

It is one thing to have confidence in yourself. It is quite another when others expect you to succeed. "It's hard to be the guy who's supposed to win every event, every time," White said. "It's a wonderful, horrible feeling, a great pressure looming."[88] That feeling can be overwhelming, and many talented athletes have folded under the pressure of others' expectations. But White has found a way to use that pressure to his advantage. He views it as a compliment—as in, everyone really believes in his ability, and he is proud that they expect greatness from him.

Not only do White's fans expect him to win, but his competitors do as well—which can make them all the more determined to make sure that he loses. In fact, some snowboarders want to beat

White more than they want to win. Part of this might be because the media often portray White as unbeatable. He knows that this is far from the truth, and so do his competitors. "I can't remember the last contest in which everyone wasn't trying to bump me off," White says. "Guys are savvy to the fact that I can be beat. They understand what gets overlooked: I'm just human."[89]

A Man in Motion

When he is not practicing or competing, White finds it difficult to just relax and enjoy himself. Part of this is because he gets such a sense of fulfillment out of pushing himself toward a goal. By alternating between snowboarding in the winter and skateboarding in the summer, he avoids having long spells of down time. White hates having nothing to do. During some free time before the 2010 Olympics, he got so restless that he nearly took a surfing trip to Hawaii—until he realized that the waves at that time of year were twenty-four-feet (7.3m) tall. "I didn't think it was a good idea to drown before the Olympics,"[90] he said.

White and Nintendo executive Cammie Dunaway demonstrate the "Shaun White Snowboarding" video game. White has also released a skateboarding game bearing his name.

He now fills the dead time between contests by throwing himself into his many entertainment projects and business ventures, insisting on being involved in every product that bears his name. He has produced several best-selling snowboarding and skateboarding video games, including the October 2010 release "Shaun White Skateboarding." White made sure that the movements of the animated skateboarders are as realistic as possible by using "motion capture," a process in which he performs actual skateboarding tricks against a green screen so that animators can transfer those movements to the characters. While promoting the game on *The Tonight Show with Jay Leno*, he admitted that his friends usually beat him at his own video games. "It's brutal," he told Leno. "I should know the magic in the game, but they play so much that they beat me as me. . . . It's the most frustrating thing ever"[91] — especially when he hears his own recorded voice say, "Take that!" when someone else beats him at the game.

White has also started a skateboard manufacturing company called Shaun White Supply Co., which aims to provide high-quality, low-cost equipment that is rider-friendly for the beginner skateboarder. He still continues to design clothing and equipment with his brother, Jesse. One of their ventures is a line of reasonably priced sports equipment and clothing for Target. The brothers had a lot of fun giving their creations names like "Puff the Magic Jacket," "Jacket of the Gods," and the "Most Unholy Jacket Ever." When asked why he chose such odd names for his clothing line, White said, "I wanted parents to have to call [Target] and ask, 'Do you have the Most Unholy Jacket Ever?'"[92]

In addition to his sports-related activities, White has also done some acting. He had a small part in the Black Keys video for the song, "Howlin' for You," and he played an obnoxious version of himself in the 2011 movie, *Friends with Benefits*. He has also become interested in performance driving. He partnered with tire company BF Goodrich in their Upgrade to BF Goodrich campaign, and a team of professional drivers trained him to drive a Vermont SportsCar rally vehicle. The look of the vehicle was designed by Jesse.

Cutting Loose

White has admitted that he enjoys being in the public spotlight, but he still wishes that he could cut loose from time to time. In 2010, he told *Rolling Stone*, "I was just in a bar in Colorado, and someone told me Hunter Thompson was sitting there once and threw a stick of dynamite behind the bar. Do you know what would happen if I did that? If I put the TV out the window right now, it would be international news."

White took very good care of his public image until September 2012, when he was arrested outside of a hotel in Nashville for vandalism and public intoxication. Police reports indicate that, after celebrating at a wedding with family and friends, White pulled a fire alarm in the hotel, causing it to be evacuated. When a citizen tried to stop him from leaving the scene, he and White had an altercation that left White with a bruise on his face, apparently caused by a fall. White posted a public apology on Facebook a few days later.

Quoted in Vanessa Grigoriadis. "Up in the Air." *Rolling Stone*, March 18, 2010.

A Budding Guitarist

Playing guitar is another way White relaxes, and it has become an important part of his life. He has always been a fan of hard rock. One of his favorite perks of celebrity is that it has given him the opportunity to meet some of his personal guitar heroes, including Slash, the former lead guitarist of Guns N' Roses. He first met Slash at the summer X Games. "I was on the vert ramp, dropping to do a run," he remembers, "and out of nowhere, as I'm skating, Slash walks out onto the ramp and starts soloing." White could not believe it was happening. When he spoke to Slash later, the musician admitted that he was just as excited to be on the ramp with White. "It's just one of those things where athletes want to be musicians and musicians want to be athletes,"[93] White said.

White jams with a band at a Sundance Film Festival event in 2009. He enjoys playing guitar to relax and have fun.

White started playing guitar when he was seventeen. At first, he got into a fierce, one-sided competition with his neighbor, who happened to be more advanced. Unbeknownst to the neighbor, White was obsessed with outplaying him, and he practiced obsessively for weeks at a time. Finally, he realized that playing guitar was not a competitive sport. He is now able to play for fun and finds it extremely relaxing. He can hold his own with a band, and he even played guitar at Jesse's wedding. "I think guitar is the best thing in the world," he told *Rolling Stone*. "It's the only thing where no matter what I do, I can't do it all myself. There's only so good you can get in your room, and it's never going to sound as rad as if I play with other people. With guitar, I really can't win."[94]

In Rwanda with Right to Play

Whether it is in sports, business, or recreation, White rarely gets involved in an activity unless it is special to him. His charity efforts are no exception. Because of the heart defect he suffered as a child, he works with several charities that promote health and fitness, including Yum-o!, which encourages healthy eating among underprivileged youth. He also supports St. Jude Children's Research Hospital in Tennessee, and has partnered with Vail Resorts to donate a portion of every ticket sold to the research hospital. St. Jude also has a long-term housing facility for the families of its patients, similar to the facility that White's family lived in when he was undergoing his surgeries as an infant. White designed and built a rock-and-roll-themed living room and playroom for the facility, complete with a foosball table and a video game area.

White also promotes skateboarding as a wonderful activity for young people, especially at-risk youth. He is grateful that there were skate parks available to him when he was growing up, and he believes that if he did not have skateboarding, he probably would have gotten into trouble. He has taken part in Stand Up For Skateparks, a celebrity benefit organized by Tony Hawk that brings free public skate parks to impoverished areas.

White attends Tony Hawk's Stand Up for Skateparks benefit in 2012. Hawk's charity is one of several that White has supported over the years.

White has taken these efforts international. After the 2006 Winter Olympics, for example, he spent a week in Rwanda with the organization Right to Play, teaching kids how to skateboard. Right to Play promotes sports in impoverished or war-torn countries as a way to encourage good nutrition and health. Rwanda is a poor country in central Africa that endured a bloody civil war and genocide in 1990, which left nearly a million people dead. On his trip, White learned much about the country's history and culture and then spent several days building skate ramps and giving school-aged children skateboarding lessons. "It was amazing," he said. "It just put me in this whole different mindset. I don't know—you see people happy when they don't have as much as you think they need. You appreciate what you have, and you appreciate that they're just as happy not having all these special things that you have."[95] The trip helped him put his own fame

The Secret to Skateboarding

While spending a week teaching children to skateboard in Rwanda, White had the opportunity to give a young boy advice about confidence and skateboarding. The boy, who had never been on a skateboard, stood out from the rest—after only a day of instruction, he was already doing simple tricks. When the day was done, the boy, speaking through a translator, asked White to tell him the secret to being a great skateboarder. White thought a minute and then said, "Tell him it's all about being confident. Really know you can do it, and it just kind of happens."

Quoted in *Shaun White: Don't Look Down*. DVD. Directed by Willie Ebersol. Santa Monica, CA: ESPN Films, 2009.

in perspective, and he was so affected by the spirit of the people he met that he sponsored a rural village and helped them build a community well.

What Is Next for the Flying Tomato?

For Shaun White, the future is still up in the air. Board sport athletes tend to peak in their mid-twenties, and while White is at the height of his athletic powers, he is gradually transitioning to life after extreme sports. At the 2012 Summer Olympics, he took his first stab at being a sports commentator for women's gymnastics. Though he admits that he does not know much about the sport, "I know what it's like to put a run together, or a routine, and how to deal with the pressure of competing and shaking it off if something goes wrong. We compete in such different sports, but

A frequent face at celebrity events, White arrives at the premiere of The Avengers *at the Tribeca Film Festival in April 2012.*

we all have so much in common."[96] He is excited that the 2014 Olympics will add a slopestyle event in snowboarding, and he plans to compete in both halfpipe and slopestyle. He would also love to compete in Olympic skateboarding if it is added to the 2016 Summer Olympics.

In his personal life, he has been dating, attending celebrity events, and enjoying his role as an extreme sports superstar. But even though his life—and the sport of snowboarding—has changed completely since those long-ago days of sleeping in a van with his family in the back of the ski resort parking lot, deep down, White still feels like one of the "sketchy snowboard kids"[97] shredding up the mountain.

Introduction: An American Icon

1. Quoted in Michelle Hurni. "Shaun White Opens Up." ESPN, January 24, 2010. http://espn.go.com/action/xgames/winter/2010/countdown/blog/_/post/4854284.

2. Quoted in Gavin Edwards. "Shaun White." Rule Forty Two (blog). http://rulefortytwo.com/articles-essays/gallimaufry/shaun-white. (Originally published in slightly shorter form as the cover story of *Rolling Stone*, March 9, 2006.)

3. Quoted in Allison Glock. "Shaun White, Snowboarding's Hottest Star, Is Set to Blow Up in Skateboarding, Too." ESPN: The Magazine, May 26, 2003. http://sports.espn.go.com/espnmag/story?id=3246499.

4. Quoted in Alyssa Roenigk. "Hard to Believe There Was a Time When Shaun White Wasn't the Biggest Thing on Olympic Snow." ESPN.com, July 10, 2012. http://sports.espn.go.com/espn/magazine/archives/news/story?page=magazine-20100222-article18.

5. Quoted in Method TV. "5 Minutes with Shaun White," March 22, 2007. www.youtube.com/watch?v=fjDt1p61dbg&list=PLE456C0A7F71C6AAF&index=2&feature=plpp_video.

Chapter 1: A Born Competitor

6. Quoted in Glock. "Shaun White, Snowboarding's Hottest Star."

7. Quoted in FM News Radio 750 KXL. "Olympian Shaun White," August 12, 2010. www.youtube.com/user/750kxl/videos?query=shaun+white.

8. Quoted in Jill Lieber. "Teen Snowboarder Chases Dreams." USA Today, January 9, 2002. www.usatoday.com/sports/olympics/saltlake/snowboard/2002-01-10-teen.htm.

9. Quoted in Rosanna Greenstreet. "Q&A: Shaun White." Life and Style. Guardian (Manchester, UK), March 12, 2010.

www.guardian.co.uk/lifeandstyle/2010/mar/13/shaun-white-interview.

10. Quoted in Vanessa Grigoriadis. "Up in the Air." Rolling Stone, March 18, 2010.

11. Quoted in David Swanson. "Shaun White Interview." Maxim. www.maxim.com/other-sports/shaun-white-interview.

12. Quoted in 60 Minutes. "White: It's Sometimes Lonely at the Top." CBS News, July 12, 2010. www.cbsnews.com/2100-18560_162-6151366.html.

13. Quoted in 60 Minutes. "White: It's Sometimes Lonely at the Top."

14. Quoted in *Sportskool: One on One with Shaun White.* HBO, 2008. Streamed online via Grace Creek Media. www.sportskool.com/sports/snowboarding.

15. Quoted in *Sportskool: One on One with Shaun White.*

16. Quoted in *Sportskool: One on One with Shaun White.*

17. Quoted in *Sportskool: One on One with Shaun White.*

18. Quoted in Peter Davis. "Future Boy: The Fast Times of Shaun White, Living Legend." Paper, February 13, 2006. www.papermag.com/arts_and_style/2006/02/future-boy.php.

19. Quoted in *Sportskool: One on One with Shaun White.*

20. Quoted in Edwards. "Shaun White."

21. Quoted in Glock. "Shaun White, Snowboarding's Hottest Star."

22. Quoted in *Sportskool: One on One with Shaun White.*

23. Quoted in *Sportskool: One on One with Shaun White.*

24. Quoted in Tom Eagar. "Shaun White Interview." Huck, October 29, 2010. www.huckmagazine.com/features/shaun-white-interview.

25. Quoted in Rick Baker. "Shaun White Interview." Pop Magazine, June 4, 2010. www.popmag.com.au/home/news/shaun-white-interview.aspx.

26. Quoted in 60 Minutes. "White: It's Sometimes Lonely at the Top."

27. Quoted in 60 Minutes. "White: It's Sometimes Lonely at the Top."

28. Quoted in 60 Minutes. "White: It's Sometimes Lonely at the Top."

29. Quoted in 60 Minutes. "White: It's Sometimes Lonely at the Top."

30. Quoted in 60 Minutes. "White: It's Sometimes Lonely at the Top."

31. Quoted in Chris Coyle. "The Shaun White Interview." TransWorld Snowboarding, October 2003. http://snowboarding .transworld.net/1000026824/uncategorized/the-shaun-white-interview.

Chapter 2: Rising Through the Ranks

32. Hans Prosl. "Powers, Thost Take Pipe." Mountainzone.com, December 5, 1999. "http://classic.mountainzone.com/snow boarding/2000/vans/breckenridge/halfpipe.html.

33. Quoted in TransWorld Snowboarding. "The Norse Conflicts: It's the 2001 Arctic Challenge," October 1, 2001. http://snow boarding.transworld.net/1000026496/other/the-norse-con flicts-its-the-2001-arctic-challenge.

34. Quoted in TransWorld Snowboarding. "The Norse Conflicts."

35. Quoted in Simon. "Shaun White Interview." Kidzworld. www .kidzworld.com/article/10362-shaun-white-interview.

36. Quoted in Sportskool: One on One with Shaun White.

37. Quoted in Sportskool: One on One with Shaun White.

38. Quoted in Lieber. "Teen Snowboarder Chases Dreams."

39. Quoted in Coyle. "The Shaun White Interview."

40. Quoted in Mark Borden. "Shaun White Lifts Off." Fast Company, January 14, 2009. www.fastcompany.com/1139303/ shaun-whites-business-red-hot.

41. Quoted in Sportskool: One on One with Shaun White.

42. Quoted in Sportskool: One on One with Shaun White.

43. Quoted in Sportskool: One on One with Shaun White.

44. Quoted in Davis. "Future Boy."

45. Quoted in Baker. "Shaun White Interview."

46. Quoted in Sportskool: One on One with Shaun White.

47. Quoted in Lieber. "Teen Snowboarder Chases Dreams."

48. Quoted in Lieber. "Teen Snowboarder Chases Dreams."

Chapter 3: The Perfect Season

49. Quoted in Glock. "Shaun White, Snowboarding's Hottest Star."
50. Quoted in Coyle. "The Shaun White Interview."
51. Quoted in *Sportskool: One on One with Shaun White.*
52. Quoted in Dave England. "Shaun White Interview." Snowboarder. www.snowboardermag.com/shaunwhite.
53. Quoted in Eagar. "Shaun White Interview."
54. Quoted in Edwards. "Shaun White."
55. Quoted in Swanson. "Shaun White Interview."
56. Quoted in Hurni. "Shaun White Opens Up."
57. Quoted in Jesse Huffman. "U.S. Snowboarding Team Coach Bud Keene Talks Shop." ESPN, December 23, 2009. http:// espn.go.com/action/snowboarding/news/story?id=4741941.
58. Quoted in Vincent Laforet. "White Spins Snowboarding Gold." New York Times, February 12, 2006. www.nytimes .com/2006/02/12/sports/olympics/12cnd-snowboarding .html?_r=0.
59. Quoted in Florence Kane. "Olympic Nostalgia: Snowboarder Shaun White." Vogue, July 24, 2012. www.vogue.com/culture/ article/olympic-nostalgia-snowboarder-shaun-white/#1.
60. Quoted in Laforet. "White Spins Snowboarding Gold."

Chapter 4: The Price of Fame

61. Quoted in Grigoriadis. "Up in the Air."
62. Quoted in *Sportskool: One on One with Shaun White.*
63. Quoted in *Sportskool: One on One with Shaun White.*
64. Quoted in Grigoriadis. "Up in the Air."
65. Quoted in *Sportskool: One on One with Shaun White.*
66. Quoted in *Shaun White: Don't Look Down.* DVD. Directed by Willie Ebersol. Santa Monica, CA: ESPN Films, 2009.
67. Quoted in *Shaun White: Don't Look Down.*
68. Quoted in *Shaun White: Don't Look Down.*
69. Quoted in *Beyond the Boundaries: 2007 Dew Tour.* TV Program. Episode 2, 2007. www.hulu.com/watch/ 21094#i0,p0,d0.

70. Quoted in *Beyond the Boundaries*.
71. Quoted in "X Games 13: Shaun White Takes Gold, PLG Second in Skate Vert Finals." Lat34.com, August 6, 2007. www.lat34.com/skate/x_games_13_skate_vert.htm.

Chapter 5: Project X

72. Quoted in Shaun White: Red Bull Project X. DVD. Directed by Sean Aaron. San Luis Obispo, CA: VAS Entertainment, 2010. www.hulu.com/shaun-white-project-x.
73. Quoted in Alyssa Roenigk. "This Is Not Shaun White." ESPN: The Magazine, January 15, 2009. http://espn.go.com/action/news/story?id=3830833.
74. Quoted in *Shaun White: Red Bull Project X*.
75. Quoted in Doug Pensinger. "For a Group of Snowboarding Pals, There's No 'I' in Friends." New York Times, March 21, 2009. www.nytimes.com/2009/03/22/sports/othersports/22frends.html.
76. Quoted in *Shaun White: Red Bull Project X*.
77. Quoted in *Shaun White: Red Bull Project X*.
78. Quoted in Jonah Lehrer. "Snowboarder Kevin Pearce's Accident." Outside, September 20, 2012. www.outsideonline.com/outdoor-adventure/athletes/Some-Reassembly-Required.html?page=all.
79. Quoted in The Oprah Winfrey Show. "Olympic Gold Medalist Shaun White on the Oprah Show!," February 22, 2010. http://mpora.com/videos/SqzENPo3i.
80. Quoted in Mr. Jones and Me. "2010 Winter Olympics: My Shaun White Interview, the Olympic Experience." Bleacher Report, February 22, 2010. http://bleacherreport.com/articles/350079-2010-winter-olympics-shaun-white-interview-the-olympic-experience.
81. Quoted in Grigoriadis. "Up in the Air."
82. Quoted in Mr. Jones and Me. "2010 Winter Olympics."

83. Quoted in Alyssa Roenigk. "White's Gold-Medal Secret? Kayaking." ESPN: The Magazine, February 18, 2010. http://sports.espn.go.com/olympics/winter/2010/snowboarding/columns/story?id=4923853.

84. Quoted in Alyssa Roenigk. "White's Gold-Medal Secret? Kayaking."

Chapter 6: What Makes Him Tick?

85. Quoted in Huffman. "U.S. Snowboarding Team Coach Bud Keene Talks Shop."

86. Quoted in Huffman. "U.S. Snowboarding Team Coach Bud Keene Talks Shop."

87. Quoted in *Shaun White: Don't Look Down.*

88. Quoted in Roenigk. "Hard to Believe There Was a Time When Shaun White Wasn't the Biggest Thing on Olympic Snow."

89. Quoted in Roenigk. "Hard to Believe There Was a Time When Shaun White Wasn't the Biggest Thing on Olympic Snow."

90. Quoted in Grigoriadis. "Up in the Air."

91. Quoted in *The Tonight Show with Jay Leno*, Season 19, Episode 13, October 6, 2010. Universal Media Studios. Big Dog Productions. www.hulu.com/watch/183860.

92. Quoted in Borden. "Shaun White Lifts Off."

93. Quoted in *Sportskool: One on One with Shaun White.*

94. Quoted in Grigoriadis. "Up in the Air."

95. Quoted in *Shaun White: Don't Look Down.*

96. Quoted in Alyssa Roenigk. "Shaun White Joins NBC for Olympic Work." July 31, 2012. ESPN.com. http://espn.go.com/blog/playbook/trending/post/_/id/5745/shaun-white-joins-nbc-for-olympics-work.

97. Quoted in Grigoriadis. "Up in the Air."

1986

Shaun Roger White is born in San Diego, California, on September 3 to Roger and Cathy White. He is diagnosed with a congenital heart condition and undergoes two open-heart surgeries in his first year of life.

1992

White learns how to skateboard and snowboard, emulating his older brother, Jesse.

1993

White's parents enter him in the Southern California Collegiate Snowsports Conference's annual amateur competition. He wins nearly every contest, progressing all the way to the nationals. He is offered a sponsorship with Burton Snowboards.

1994

White wins the Collegiate Snowsports Conference's national championship. It is his first of five consecutive conference wins.

1995

White meets Tony Hawk at the Encinitas YMCA skate park. Hawk begins to mentor him in skateboarding.

1997

White is nearly killed in a skateboarding accident at the 1997 MTV Sports and Music Festival, colliding with pro skater Bob Burnquist and sustaining a fractured skull.

1999

At thirteen, White turns pro. He places tenth in his first professional contest. That season he competes in snowboarding competitions all over the world.

2000

White wins his first professional contest, the Arctic Challenge in Norway. His family moves up the coast to Carlsbad, California, so that White can attend a more flexible school.

2001

Tony Hawk sponsors White in skateboarding. White begins to tour with Hawk's company, Birdhouse Skateboards.

2002

White misses making the U.S. Olympic snowboarding team by three-tenths of a point.

2003

White wins his first double gold at the winter X Games, coming in first in both slopestyle and halfpipe. That summer, he turns pro in skateboarding, coming in fourth in his first professional competition. He is invited to the summer X Games and places sixth in vert skating.

2004

White tears the meniscus in his right knee and has to sit out most of the season.

2006

White has a perfect season in snowboarding, wining every contest he enters. He travels to Turin, Italy, for the Winter Olympics and brings home the gold medal.

2007

After a lackluster snowboard season, White travels to Rwanda to work with the organization Right to Play. Later that summer, he wins the summer X Games gold medal in vert skateboarding. He becomes the first athlete in the history of the X Games to compete in both the summer and winter X Games in the same year.

2009

In February, Red Bull builds White a halfpipe in a secret location in the Colorado Rockies so that White can teach himself double cork maneuvers in preparation for the 2010 Olympics. He unveils his new tricks at the Burton Open in New Zealand.

2010

White wins his second gold medal at the 2010 Winter Olympics in Vancouver, Canada. He holds the record for the highest Olympic score in the halfpipe competition. That summer he is undefeated on the Dew Tour, winning his second Dew Cup for vert skating.

2012

White wins his fifth consecutive gold medal in the halfpipe competition at the winter X Games. He is awarded the first perfect score in the history of the competition.

For More Information

Books

Tony Hawk and Sean Mortimer. *Tony Hawk: Professional Skateboarder*. New York: It Books: 2002. In this young adult autobiography, Tony Hawk shares the stories from his life that have helped him become a skateboarding legend.

Mike Kennedy. *Today's Superstars: Shaun White*. New York: Gareth Stevens, 2009. Appropriate for young readers, this book presents a lot of relevant information on Shaun White.

Cindy Kleh. *Being a Snowboarder*. Minneapolis: Lerner, 2012. This title explores how to become a professional snowboarder. Includes a glossary of snowboard lingo, as well as highlights of notable people in the world of snowboarding.

Periodicals

Mark Borden. "Shaun White Lifts Off." *Fast Company*, January 14, 2009.

Chris Coyle. "The Shaun White Interview." *TransWorld Snowboarding*, October 2003.

Elliot David. "Watch the Throne." *V*, Spring 2012.

Peter Davis. "Future Boy: The Fast Times of Shaun White, Living Legend." *Paper*, February 13, 2006.

Tom Eagar. "Shaun White Interview." *Huck*, October 29, 2010.

Gavin Edwards. "Shaun White." *Rolling Stone*, March 9, 2006.

Allison Glock. "Shaun White, Snowboarding's Hottest Star, Is Set to Blow Up in Skateboarding, Too." *ESPN: The Magazine*, May 26, 2003.

Rosanna Greenstreet. "Q&A: Shaun White." Life and Style. *Guardian* (Manchester, UK), March 12, 2010.

Vanessa Grigoriadis. "Up in the Air." *Rolling Stone*, March 18, 2010.

Vincent Laforet. "White Spins Snowboarding Gold." *New York Times*, February 12, 2006.

Jill Lieber. "Teen Snowboarder Chases Dreams." *USA Today*, January 9, 2002.

Alyssa Roenigk. "White's Gold-Medal Secret? Kayaking." *ESPN: The Magazine*, February 18, 2010.

Internet Sources

Jesse Huffman. "U.S. Snowboarding Team Coach Bud Keene Talks Shop." ESPN, December 23, 2009. http://espn.go.com/action/snowboarding/news/story?id=4741941.

Michelle Hurni. "Shaun White Opens Up." *ESPN*, January 24, 2010. http://espn.go.com/action/xgames/winter/2010/count-down/blog/_/post/4854284.

Documentaries

Shaun White: Don't Look Down. DVD. Directed by Willie Ebersol. Santa Monica, CA: ESPN Films, 2009.

Shaun White: Red Bull Project X. DVD. Directed by Sean Aaron. San Luis Obispo, CA: VAS Entertainment, 2010.

Sportskool: One on One with Shaun White. HBO, 2008. Streamed online via Grace Creek Media. www.sportskool.com/sports/snowboarding.

Picture Credits

About the Author

Christine Wilcox studied literature at Temple University and received an MA in English from the University of Maine. Her other contribution to Lucent's People in the News series is *Justin Bieber*. Wilcox lives in Richmond, Virginia, with her husband, David, and her stepson, Anthony.